Cambridge Elements

Elements in Historical Theory and Practice
edited by
Daniel Woolf
Queen's University, Ontario

THE TRANSFORMATION OF HISTORICAL RESEARCH IN THE DIGITAL AGE

Ian Milligan
University of Waterloo

CAMBRIDGE
UNIVERSITY PRESS

Shaftesbury Road, Cambridge CB2 8EA, United Kingdom

One Liberty Plaza, 20th Floor, New York, NY 10006, USA

477 Williamstown Road, Port Melbourne, VIC 3207, Australia

314–321, 3rd Floor, Plot 3, Splendor Forum, Jasola District Centre,
New Delhi – 110025, India

103 Penang Road, #05–06/07, Visioncrest Commercial, Singapore 238467

Cambridge University Press is part of Cambridge University Press & Assessment,
a department of the University of Cambridge.

We share the University's mission to contribute to society through the pursuit of
education, learning and research at the highest international levels of excellence.

www.cambridge.org
Information on this title: www.cambridge.org/9781009012522

DOI: 10.1017/9781009026055

First published 2022

A catalogue record for this publication is available from the British Library.

ISBN 978-1-009-01252-2 Paperback
ISSN 2634-8616 (online)
ISSN 2634-8608 (print)

Cambridge University Press & Assessment has no responsibility for the persistence
or accuracy of URLs for external or third-party internet websites referred to in this
publication and does not guarantee that any content on such websites is, or will
remain, accurate or appropriate.

The Transformation of Historical Research in the Digital Age

Elements in Historical Theory and Practice

DOI: 10.1017/9781009026055
First published online: August 2022

Ian Milligan
University of Waterloo

Author for correspondence: Ian Milligan, i2millig@uwaterloo.ca

Abstract: Historians make research queries on Google, ProQuest, and the HathiTrust. They garner information from keyword searches, carried out across millions of documents, their research shaped by algorithms they rarely understand. Historians often then visit archives in whirlwind trips marked by thousands of digital photographs, subsequently explored on computer monitors from the comfort of their offices. They may then take to social media or other digital platforms, their work shaped through these new forms of pre- and post-publication review. Almost all aspects of the historian's research workflow have been transformed by digital technology. In other words, *all* historians – not just Digital Historians – are implicated in this shift. *The Transformation of Historical Research in the Digital Age* equips historians to be *self-conscious* practitioners by making these shifts explicit and exploring their long-term impact. This title is also available as Open Access on Cambridge Core.

Keywords: historical methods, digital history, digital humanities, digital publishing, history in the digital age

ISBNs: 9781009012522 (PB), 9781009026055 (OC)
ISSNs: 2634-8616 (online), 2634-8608 (print)

Contents

1 Introduction

Over a generation of historical scholarship, the way in which historians research and write has dramatically changed. While many of these changes have been individually small, cumulatively they represent a transformation in the way that historical scholarship is researched, written, and published. These changes have been seldom theorized or explicitly discussed.[1] Younger historians may not know what research was like before the Internet, important when they critique earlier scholarship. Older historians have experienced a process that eludes comprehension, as everyday interactions with the Internet shape how they search and engage with sources. Historians must take stock of just how drastically technology has transformed their scholarship.

Imagine a historian researching in the year 2000. The historian would first choose a project, explore the secondary literature, and then find primary sources of interest by looking at what other scholars had cited or by phoning or arranging interviews with subject-specialist archivists.[2] They might even consult massive tomes which aggregated available resources and listed archival repositories. The historian would then travel to the archive, perhaps carrying out some photocopying (at expensive prices of 25 cents a page or more), but would primarily carry out in situ research: taking notes on a (still-then bulky and expensive) laptop computer or notepad. This archival work would be complemented by microfilm work, either in the archive or at home thanks to the inter-library loan of reels: day after day of scrolling through microfilm reels, painstaking work that incidentally also exposed the historian to rich historical context. While what had been microfilmed reflected the biases of a previous generation, the way in which a historian manually explored documents resembled earlier paper-based exploration.

Historical research in 2000 was slow and laborious compared to today. This was thanks to the considerable outlay of time to navigate information and the specialized expertise to triage and search it effectively. Archives were chosen sparingly, microfilm reels with care, reflecting the intensive labour needed to explore these repositories of information. This is not to paint an unduly utopian situation. Archives have always varied in their accessibility (hours, location), organizational acuity (funding and comprehensiveness), and beyond. Crucially too, while the year 2000 is posited for the purposes of this thought experiment, it could just as easily be 1990 or 1980. The changes over the last two decades have been dramatic.

---

[1] See important treatments in Hitchcock, 'Confronting the Digital'; Putnam, 'Transnational and the Text-Searchable'; Jordanova, *History in Practice*; Milligan, 'Illusionary Order'. Crymble, *Technology and the Historian* puts much of this into historical context.

[2] Canonical works on the historian's craft include Tosh, *Pursuit of History*; Marius and Page, *Short Guide to Writing about History*; Storey and Jones, *Writing History*.

Fast-forward to the present day and historical research is carried out very differently. Comparing these two historical workflows is useful to see just how dramatically historical research has changed.[3] At 40,000 feet it may look the same. Historians identify problems, find sources, study them, and publish. But the detailed on-the-ground work of a historian has undergone a digital revolution.

Historical research in the digital age begins in familiar fashion: choosing a project and exploring the historiography. Yet the way in which a historian finds primary archival sources is very different: Google searches for archives, consulting archival websites, and navigating extensive digitized finding aids. At all stages, the historian balances what *is* and what is *not* digitized. This was in play with microfilm too – what was and was not filmed – but more material was microfilmed than is currently digitized. Some archives are still worth traveling to, but there is a different and new cost–benefit analysis at play. Online resources are consulted more, the non-digitized less, a historical application of the 'Matthew Effect' where the digitized get richer (in citations) and the non-digitized poorer.[4] Given the high cost of digitization, this process tends to – some projects have consciously tried to counter this trend – privilege sources held by affluent institutions across the Global North, with implications for the ensuing diversity of voices and perspectives in our scholarship.[5] While many of these shifts build on pre-digital trends, historical information is always mediated, whether this is due to the choice of what to microfilm or to broader archival biases – yet the transformation of the digital age represents a dramatic acceleration.

Historical information is mediated through new and emerging technology. When a historian does travel to an archive, their reading room activity is different than what it would have been just two decades ago. Trips are quicker, with the scholar standing over archival fonds with digital camera in hand, collecting thousands of photographs (along with incidental back pain). The historian does most of their actual reading and analysis at home.[6] The same is true with other periodicals, newspapers, and journals: historians explore large repositories of information, from places such as JSTOR, ProQuest, or HathiTrust, through the constant lens of search. They use keywords rather than expert indexes. Here too historians find themselves consulting the digitized

---

[3] For an earlier exploration of the transformation of historical research, see Rutner and Schonfeld, 'Supporting the Changing Research Practices of Historians'.

[4] Hitchcock, 'Confronting the Digital'; Milligan, 'Illusionary Order'.

[5] Global North refers to the grouping of affluent countries, primarily but not exclusively in the North (one would include Australia and New Zealand in the Global North), who control the majority of the world's earned income.

[6] Milligan, 'We Are All Digital Now'.

rather than what might be most relevant. This is not out of laziness, but rather the diminished returns of consulting a newspaper that is not digitized while a roughly equivalent periodical might be. It might not seem like a significant decision to explore the *Toronto Star* rather than the *Toronto Telegraph*, but if every historian makes the same decision, this represents a dramatic shift. These thousands of individual decisions mean that over time scholarship begins to homogenize in terms of what we cite. While these forces are most pronounced for historians who draw on typeset documents – those most amenable to optical character recognition algorithms – recent advances in handwritten text recognition also portend the continuing expansion of technology's impact. While microfilm had the effect to some degree on an earlier generation of scholars, digitization is so much more circumscribed – and its access via keywords represents a change of an entirely different magnitude.

The possibilities offered by digital sources came to the forefront of many historians' minds during the prolonged COVID-19 pandemic. With reading rooms closed, travel restricted, and physical access to libraries intermittent during various waves of lockdowns and restrictions, historians adapted as best they could. Historical scholarship was impacted (also by increased caregiver responsibilities and the pandemic's trauma itself), but thanks to digital media, in general research did not come to a complete standstill in most cases. Many historians continued to research. As with everything, COVID accelerated but did not invent trends: it underscored how digitally mediated historical scholarship now is. Historians were able to leverage processes that had been unfolding over decades.

This dramatic transformation has unfolded over the span of two decades.[7] It is difficult to think of a single element of a historian's research workflow that has not changed over this period. We look at old acknowledgements and remark on how they underscore the research practices of a past generation: the wife of a famous historian who apparently did all their work, or a scholar who churlishly 'dis-acknowledges' an archive. But they are windows into how work is carried out.[8] These transformative forces are accelerating, especially as historians begin to leverage the vast arrays of born-digital sources (those that begin life as digital objects, such as a website or a Word document) that will reshape the landscape of historical records for topics studying the 1990s and beyond. Indeed, this was the subject of my last book.[9] But the forces described in this Element are applicable to more historians than just the (current) minority drawing on born-digital sources. Indeed, an understanding of how historical

---

[7]   Cohen and Rosenzweig, *Digital History;* Weller, *History in the Digital Age*; Jordanova, *History in Practice.*

[8]   Callaci, 'On Acknowledgements'.   [9]   Milligan, *History in the Age of Abundance?*

work has been transformed is especially important as historians tend to neglect methodological discussion. Let us explore these transformations – and learn how we can be better scholars by making the digital explicit.

1.1 The Transformation of Historical Scholarship

This Element explores how this technological transformation has unfolded and what its impact will be. Yet it is not a 'how-to' guide.[10] This Element rather explores how this digital turn is changing historical scholarship and practice. The public – and even some historians – can sometimes see historical scholarship as 'objective'. From this perspective, archives are understood as passing along to historians stories from the past from which they write history.[11] Yet historians are of course influenced by their working conditions. Do they read documents on a screen or not? Can they access funding to travel to the archives that they want to? Do they have technical ability and knowledge to understand the knowledge systems they are using? Can they understand how to conduct keyword searches properly, do they grasp the underlying constraints of optical character recognition (OCR) in the database they are searching, or grasp what was or what was *not* digitized? Do they have children, constraining working hours or travel opportunities (making databases an especial godsend)? Are they in the developing world and accessing a website too overbuilt for their tenuous internet connection? All these mundane questions shape historical scholarship.

This transformation is neither wholly negative nor positive. Few revolutionary shifts are. Gains include rapid access to sources, quick fact-checking, the ability to search over decades and continents of historical sources, and – significantly – the ability to spend more time with family, teaching, and other duties and less time in faraway archives scribbling in notepads. The democratizing potential of these shifts cannot be ignored. Similarly, historians can use keyword search to amass large corpora of information. They now generally operate on new, larger bodies of information. Yet there are losses. Notably, historians can lose an understanding of historical context when keyword-searching directly to sentences or individual documents removed from their broader context. Historians are also using information retrieval systems that are not understood, the contents of which are in turn shaped by digitization bias. Similarly, this new scope of digitized research brings advantages and disadvantages. Search brings us many more results, but we still tend

---

[10] For a 'how-to' guide, see Graham, Milligan, and Weingart, *Exploring Big Historical Data*.

[11] For the canonical overview of objectivity and the historical profession, see Novick, *That Noble Dream*. On archives, I am convinced by Alexandra Walsham's argument that historians tend to treat archives as 'neutral and unproblematic reservoirs of historical fact'. See Walsham, 'Social History of the Archive'.

to evaluate research claims on a pre-digital level of sourcing.[12] As historians now systematically explore thousands of articles with algorithms, perhaps our norms need to change and now require a half-dozen or more 'hits' to rise to the same level of significance we might have looked for in a pre-digital period. The way in which we evaluate scholarship via peer-review and scholarly assessment also need to take this new information ecosystem into account.

Sitting at a computer all day also represents significant change in how historians approach their research questions. We are perhaps losing the experiential knowledge of a place at a time when parts of our profession are underscoring the importance of community and place-based research. Yet there is no going back; the digital genie is out of the bottle. Whether this transformation is positive or not depends in no small part on the critical ardour with which historians approach their digitally transformed world.

Through careful and critical use of digital technologies we can ensure that this transformation is a net gain. Issues of context present the biggest challenges. Most digital systems are not designed to reveal context and are instead focused on keyword search. With better training and conscious digital research methods, however, we can countenance this to some degree. This may also require a collective change in the ways in which historians approach the level of citation needed to establish a scholarly claim, thanks to the larger amounts of information that we all increasingly operate on. With more user demand, more platforms can adopt an approach which facilitates context-aware reading, an approach adopted by the Internet Archive. Digital historians have also pushed the literature forward on the provision of context, informing primary documents through network analysis and trends.[13] Experiential knowledge also raises questions, requiring a deeper conversation about what we as a profession value. As a self-governing profession regulated primarily through peer review, we can collectively choose the direction that we want historical scholarship to go and what our values are.

This will require a transformation of our profession in four main ways, explored in this Element's conclusion. These are a recognition of digital literacy's importance, valuing interdisciplinarity, a prioritization of methodological discussions, and changing how we train future historians to incorporate new and emerging technologies. Despite the challenge before us, historians have a good foundation, especially vis-à-vis our use of context, by which to rise to these challenges.

---

[12] Underwood, 'Theorizing Research Practices', 66.
[13] Robertson and Mullen, 'Arguing with Digital History', 1030.

1.2 The Structure of this Element

This Element brings the conversation around the transformation of historical scholarship together into a sustained micro-monograph. Its goal is to equip historians to be *self-conscious* practitioners in a digital age. The Element will do so through three substantive sections after this introductory one, followed by a substantive conclusion.

The second section, 'Libraries and Databases', explores how aggressive digitization, especially of newspapers and microfilmed resources, has created massive exploratory databases. Historians need to think about their construction and explore these platforms consciously. Algorithmic bias and selective digitization practices have comprehensively transformed how historians parse information. How has everyday technology transformed the work of historians, from 1930s microfilm to twenty-first century databases? We have gained dramatic access to primary sources, but historians need to ask questions about what has been digitized, and what has not? *How* has something been digitized? What are the impacts of copyright on these repositories?

The third section, 'Archives and Access', explores the long, intertwined existence between archives and historians with special focus on digital technology and source mediation. Historians are expert users of archives, although growing estrangement has led scholars increasingly to consider the interactions between the two parties as 'interdisciplinary' encounters.[14] This section thus explores how technology has changed the relationship between historian, archivist, and archives. What has the impact of partial collection digitization been? Online finding aids? Digital photography? Over the last two decades, historians are spending less time than ever before in archives, yet never have we had such powerful tools and platforms at our disposal.

The fourth section, 'Publishing in an Interdisciplinary Age: From Journal to Social Media', explores the changing relationship between historians and their audiences. When historians think of 'digital history', many think of digital public history, thanks to the historical profession's long lineage of public-facing engagement.[15] Public scholarship has taken the shape of CD-ROMs, exhibit sites, 'memory banks', social media, and engagement on Wikipedia. Yet traditional career progression – hiring, and in North America, tenure and promotion – compel scholars towards traditional markers of career success as embodied in certain publication types (especially traditional books). How has technology changed publishing? This section briefly explores new formats, the

---

[14] Blouin and Rosenberg, *Processing the Past*, 10.
[15] See Brennan, 'Public, First'; Robertson, 'Differences between Digital Humanities and Digital History'.

changing approaches towards idea circulation, and the potential for interdisciplinary engagement.

Historians have rarely been transparent enough about many of the above topics: we treat scholarship as finished products, and methods are too often relegated to footnotes or informal discussions.[16] We could all do better history by reflecting on the ongoing technological transformation that is changing how we research.

1.3 Are We All Digital Historians Now? Digital History and the Digital Humanities

Scholars have been exploring how to explicitly use new and emerging technologies for humanistic and historical research since the 1950s and 1960s, under the auspices of what we today call the Digital Humanities or more specifically Digital History. The relationship between these two DHs is complicated. Digital History owes its lineage both to the Digital Humanities *and also* to currents and trends within the broader historical profession, particularly public history.

The Digital Humanities, broadly defined, explore the intersection of technology and the humanities.[17] In many ways, as Adam Crymble has explored at length, the Digital Humanities grows out of a digital literary studies tradition (by way of the Text Encoding Initiative and humanities computing scholars).[18] Historians have traditionally been underrepresented within the broad scope of the Digital Humanities and its earlier intellectual approaches.[19]

Digital History can be expansively defined as the intersection of historical scholarship with new and emerging technology. In practice, this can be broken into two subfields. First, some Digital Historians use technology to reach new and different *audiences* with new media, continuing a lineage of historians using new media to carry out the mission of social and public history. An understanding of the democratizing potential of technology has been foundational to this approach.[20] Secondly, other Digital Historians have used technology to *do* historical scholarship.[21] These scholars in part emerged from earlier approaches to quantitative history and historical demography – Social Science

---

[16] As well articulated in Arguing with Digital History Workshop, 'Digital History and Argument'.

[17] Defining the digital humanities is a topic that has filled up entire volumes. See the *Debates in Digital Humanities* series published by the University of Minnesota Press.

[18] Crymble, *Technology and the Historian*, 29.

[19] There are exceptions, of course. Canadian digital historian Chad Gaffield, for example, was awarded the Association of Digital Humanities' Organization's Antonio Zampolli Prize – the organization's highest award – in 2012.

[20] Crymble, *Technology and the Historian*, ch. 2.

[21] The focus of Graham, Milligan, and Weingart, *Exploring Big Historical Data*.

historians – as well as a smaller group of historians influenced by the more literary-focused computational studies approaches.[22]

Today, Digital Historians engage in a wide variety of scholarship. They may write programs or leverage computational platforms to assemble sources en masse, such as from records housed at the Internet Archive or the Library of Congress. Data are analysed by extracting features (i.e., word frequency, detected items in images, place names) before being subsequently analysed and visualized in a variety of ways.[23] Other Digital Historians challenge conventional norms of scholarship, exploring new methods of scholarly communication. While it is impossible to do justice to this field in a few sentences, it is a vibrant subfield adopting explicit new methodologies and approaches.

Yet what about other historians who use computers to do their work but who do not fall into the above categories? Historians now all use databases, run keyword searches across millions of documents, and take digital cameras to turn scholarly documents into electronic files to be analysed at home. Are we now all digital historians?

There is a fruitful distinction to be made between Digital History – the delineated field of study bounded by academic journals, conferences, and pedagogical approaches – and 'digitized history', or the broader transformation prompted by technology. We are not all *Digital Historians* (my capitalization is deliberate). But we all engage with digitized sources and workflows. It is unwise to silo historical engagement with technology as a subfield given its sweeping impact on the entire profession. A focus on Digital History can make the rest of the historical profession think that 'we are not digital historians', as they fire up their web browsers and research over the Internet. We are all digital now.

1.4 The Digitally Aware Historian

Let me close this introduction on an optimistic note by imagining a digitally aware historian who takes the content of this Element to heart. What kind of work would a historian who was fully cognizant of the work that technology was playing in mediating their work do?

They begin to research their topic in a newspaper database. But rather than haphazard keyword searches, they instead look at which newspapers and years are included in the database – and which ones are not. They then explicitly consider selection bias (why was *this* newspaper digitized but not *that* one) and do some contextual research on the period's newspapers. Perhaps at the end of the day they believe that the accessible advantages of the digitized newspapers

---

[22] Crymble, *Technology and the Historian*, 44–5.
[23] See an overview in Romein et al., 'State of the Field'.

outweigh the limitations of their selectivity bias, and accordingly write a few sentences to that effect in their introduction. This sets the tone for their engagement with sources throughout their manuscript. The historian thinks about what is present and what is missing. For an event, they go page-by-page for a few weeks before and after the event, developing a contextual sense of the source as well as to ensure that the OCR has not missed salient keywords. Scholarship is still assisted by databases, but every step is deliberate and thoughtful. When a button in the interface is clicked, it is done so deliberately. The database is no longer a black box.

The time then comes to work with other digitized primary sources, and many of the same questions come to the historian's mind: what's there? What's not there? They respectfully email an archival colleague and ask these questions. The sources that are used are deliberately framed and contextualized. They understand their sources and are self-reflective about their use.

The historian then goes to the archive. They anticipate a follow-up archival trip, to follow theoretical rabbit holes that will inevitably arise when looking through their digitized photographs at home after their trip. As they leave the archive, they offer to share photographs with the archive as well in case it might help. After finishing their research, they tweet about their work, think about primary sources, and are transparent in their writing about argument, method, and approach.

Maybe they will become a Digital Historian. This could entail adopting new analytical lenses, moving away from the typical approach of 'close reading' to one of distant reading. Alternatively, they could draw on metadata to visualize interconnections between sources, or challenge norms of scholarship by publishing a database, a map, or another novel form of scholarly communication. New frontiers may then present themselves. But most historians will not go down this route. Instead, what we have seen in the above hypothetical of a digitally conscious researcher is one that pays heed to the mediating influence of technology on their work. The researcher understands that the way by which sources are mediated has had profound impact on how they are read, understood, and contextualized. In short, this is a digitally-aware historian, actively using technology rather than being shaped by it.

2 Libraries and Databases

The 1990s witnessed the rise of primary source mass digitization projects. Building upon the intellectual foundation provided by earlier projects, such as Project Gutenberg (a volunteer book transcription effort dating back to 1971 and the ARPANET), by the 1990s there were projects such as the Library of Congress' American Memory Project, American historian Ed Ayers' pathbreaking web-based Valley of the Shadow civil war document compendium, and the pioneering *Who Built America?* Textbook and primary source reader which, for a time, was included with every Apple Computer.[24] Yet this early wave was limited, compared to what was set to come by the first decade of the twenty-first century. Technology in the 1990s was insufficient for the task of mass digitization. Transcription projects were limited due to the effort of typing everything. Taking digital photographs of primary documents to share was hampered by comparatively low-quality and expensive digital cameras, limited storage, and bandwidth limitations (by today's standards). Sharing high-quality photographs was not possible at any real scale until widespread high-speed Internet (a factor to which we will return, as there are still access issues today in much of the world). Early projects made it clear that there was an interest in both providing material and using it, but the 1990s state of technology did not yet allow for mass digitization.

All of that would quickly change at the dawn of the twenty-first century. Large arrays of digitized sources were created, both directly and via the scanning of microfilm, and transformed historical scholarship. We need to understand the implications of this process, including the ultimate impact on historical scholarship of these multi-layered primary source repositories. A dive into these databases, from their historical roots to the layers that comprise them today, helps historians gain an essential understanding of how their sources are mediated in the digital age.

2.1 The Microfilm Revolution

Perhaps the best parallel to our contemporary moment is the early-twentieth century move to store documents on microfilm. Indeed, microfilm in the 1930s raised utopian hopes around universal access to all knowledge, as well as its long-term stewardship and preservation.[25] Yet reception by historians was mixed. While many historians recognized the value of having sources conveniently microfilmed, others complained about eyestrain and research difficulties.[26] An understanding of this earlier moment, especially given the roots of digitization in earlier microfilming projects, lays the foundation for thinking about libraries and databases today.

Microfilms are scaled-down documents on film strip. Documents are reduced to roughly 1/25th of their original size, and then viewed through microfilm viewers which both illuminate and magnify them to original (or larger) size.

---

[24] Crymble, *Technology and the Historian*, 51–60; Cohen and Rosenzweig, *Digital History*.

[25] Discussed in Gitelman, *Paper Knowledge*. See also the array of primary documents at www.wallandbinkley.com/rcb/.

[26] Steig, 'Information Needs of Historians'.

Microfilm is a beautiful system for information retrieval. Indeed, of all the rooms in a modern research library, the highest volume of analogue information is found in the microfilm room. Entire print runs of government documents, newspapers, print repositories, and dissertations from around the world are available for immediate consultation. A run of the *New York Times* from its 1851 founding to present would fill a small warehouse. In microfilm format, it occupies a shelf or two.[27] Importantly, properly stored microfilm reels have a long lifespan, and they can be accessed with any combination of magnification and illumination.

Despite this power, in an age of instant search-and-retrieval, microfilm seems increasingly antiquated. Priceless cultural heritage sits on microfilm reels, inaccessible by contemporary standards. They are separate from where we expect to find information: the Internet. In 2021, after our library had been closed to on-site access at the University of Waterloo for a year owing to the global pandemic, I asked our library staff how many requests they had received to use the microfilm machines. The answer: one student, who happened to be doing her doctorate with me. Among over 40,000 students and over 1,300 faculty members, only one request for this treasure trove of information had been made. Times have certainly changed.

Microfilm originally promised democratic access to all information.[28] While a nineteenth-century technology, it was in the early twentieth century when – thanks in part to the work of technologist Robert C. Binkley – microfilm began to be seen as a scholarly solution to the problems of needing to expensively travel to access scarce source information.[29] In the 1920 and 1930s, the American Library of Congress microfilmed millions of documents held by the British Library, and brought them back to Washington, DC. An American researcher could now do research without crossing the Atlantic. During the Second World War, microfilm was used to facilitate transatlantic correspondence, as well as to courier secrets.[30] Microfilm hit a conceptual pinnacle in 1945, when Vannevar Bush – the American inventor and then head of the United States' Office of Scientific Research and Development – articulated his microfilm-driven 'Memex' machine in a famous *Atlantic Monthly* article.[31] The Memex, conceived in part to harness

---

[27] The field of microfilm does not have a robust literature. One exception is the controversial Baker, *Double Fold*, which viewed microfilm as a practice endangering priceless original copies.

[28] See Binkley, *Manual on Methods;* Luther, *Microfilm*.

[29] I see parallels with the invention of the printing press which also reduced the need for scholars to spend so much of their time traveling from library to library to consult books. See the overview in Eisenstein, *Printing Press as an Agent of Change*.

[30] Auerbach and Gitelman, 'Microfilm, Containment, and the Cold War'.

[31] Bush, 'As We May Think'.

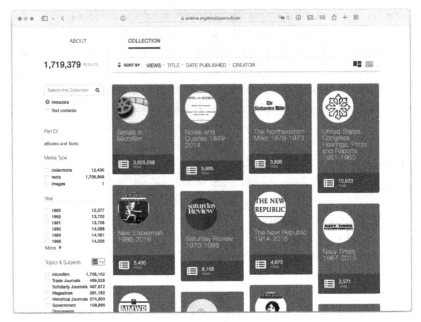

Figure 1 The Internet Archive periodical collection
(https://archive.org/details/periodicals)

the revolutionary potential of microfilm-based information, would inspire the idea of hypertext – foundational to today's World Wide Web.[32]

In other words, the advantages of making information accessible were clear. You can see what this looked like in Figure 1, a collection of digitized microfilm reels held by the Internet Archive that illustrates the production quality and scope. Researchers could go to their local university library or a major public library and consult millions of otherwise-inaccessible documents. Microfilm is a beautiful analogue system and led to a moment of massive excitement: the idea that mass amounts of information could be universally accessible.[33] But what happened to the promise of microfilm? Two factors help explain why it fell a bit short of utopian projections.

First, microfilm is difficult to use. If you have not used a microfilm machine before, imagine watching a long streaming video that you want to find a particular scene in. However, you can only press play, fast-forward, and fast-rewind. You might fast-forward too quickly, then you need to go back, and then forward, until you find the content you are looking for. Now, of course, imagine that these are thousands of individual pages that you are skimming through, and

---

[32] Milligan, *History in the Age of Abundance?*, 42–4; Barnet, *Memory Machines*, ch. 2.
[33] Gavin, 'How to Think about EEBO'.

you can see how this would quickly frustrate. With more modern digital microfilm readers, while they are generally more pleasant to use, content is also often taken out of focus while one fast-forwards and rewinds, making it difficult to read headlines when the reel is in motion.

This problem was in part what underpinned Bush's conceptual Memex. He imagined the revolutionary potential of being able to unlock the power of microfilm by quickly navigating to and displaying material of interest. The Memex envisioned the rapid retrieval and projection of microfilm within a user's desk – one would make an inquiry and the material would whirl – and pop! – immediately appear.[34] Yet these rapid retrieval systems for microfilm never came to fruition, now having largely been eclipsed by the digital turn.

Secondly, and perhaps as a portent of what would come later with digitization, microfilm was largely commercialized by a handful of big corporations. 'All' of the world's information was not microfilmed in one utopian push, but rather microfilms were increasingly produced so that they could be sold to libraries – an important distinction. While early microfilm pioneer Robert C. Binkley saw the democratizing potential of microfilm – facilitating cheap, widely distributed copies and lowering publishing costs – salesman Eugene Power saw the commercial potential of microfilm and envisioned the market for selling entire periodical runs to libraries.[35] Internet Archive founder Brewster Kahle notes that this 'transformed small libraries into holders of collections that only the largest libraries could dream of'.[36]

Commercial imperatives and historical legacies dictated choices; however, something especially important today as yesterday's microfilms often serve as the foundation of today's mass digitization projects. This is perhaps best encapsulated by Kirschenbaum and Werner's warning that the digital is a 'frankly messy complex of extensions and extrusions of prior media and technologies'.[37] As Stephen H. Gregg has shown in a recent Element on the history of the Eighteenth-Century Collections Online, this important database (published by Gale) owes its own provenance to decisions made earlier. It was a 1970s digital book cataloguing project that led into a 1980s–2000s microfilming initiative which then evolved into today's online database.[38] The same is true of periodical collections. Consider the case of Victorian periodicals. What we have today was shaped by forces including initial accessibility decisions, the

---

[34] Bush, 'As We May Think'.   [35] Power with Anderson, *Edition of One*, 154–7.
[36] Kahle, 'Microfilm'.
[37] Kirschenbaum and Werner, 'Digital Scholarship', 408, as cited in Gregg, *Old Books and Digital Publishing*, 1. Gregg is available at www.cambridge.org/core/elements/old-books-and-digital-publishing-eighteenthcentury-collections-online/058DB12DE06A4C00770B46DCFAE1D25E.
[38] Gregg, *Old Books and Digital Publishing*.

impact of the London Blitz, and which were selected for microfilming in the postwar period. All of this together decides what is digitized today.[39]

The commercial and scholarly landscape for microfilming has naturally transformed in the digital age. While a boon for libraries, Power's company – University Microfilms – was later acquired by Xerox, and then Bell & Howell, to become publishing behemoth ProQuest (in turn acquired by information conglomerate Clarivate in 2021). Databases became ProQuest's priority, microfilm became yesterday's technology, and the company's massive array of microfilmed cultural heritage was neglected. Microfilm's transformation from revolutionary technology to mundane background object helps obscure the pivotal role it played in democratizing and facilitating access to knowledge.

Even in the twenty-first century, the ability to go into the microfilm room and scroll through thousands of pages of documents continues to be a boon for scholarship. While microfilm revolutionized access by bringing documents to the scholar rather than requiring them to travel to the archives themselves, it did not dramatically change the ways in which scholars worked with documents. Microfilms are read page-by-page. A scholar advances the reels forward rather than flipping pages, but still has eyes on all of the information as it flows by. In this respect, microfilm was a less radical transformation than the keyword-search-based databases that followed.

Microfilm illustrates that the mediation of historical sources through technology has a long history: projects became feasible thanks to microfilm, and undoubtedly sources were selected depending on whether they had been put onto reels. The historical profession constantly engages *with* and is shaped *by* new and emerging technologies. In most cases, after an initial flurry of debate, new technologies become commonplace and unremarkable. Few historians had spirited debates about the role of microfilm by the middle to the late twentieth century – we just used it. Microfilm became part of the background of scholarship, machines used in the library basement without thinking, even as the reels profoundly changed the ways in which scholars chose and researched topics. The selection bias in what was microfilmed also played an important and often unrecognized role in shaping scholarship as it would serve as the basis of many digitization projects. Just because it became commonplace does not mean that its revolutionary impact was muted.

2.2 The Digitization Explosion

Two major features arrived in the late 1990s and early 2000s that dramatically changed the relationship between historians and primary sources. The first was

---

[39] Fyfe, 'Archeology'.

the advent of optical character recognition and searchable historical databases, much of which was created by scanning microfilm en masse. The second was the advent of personal digital photography, which transformed archival trips from lengthier *in situ* experiences to short gathering missions followed by the actual reading of photographed documents at home. Combined, these two factors represent dramatic change in the day-to-day research workflows of historians.

Optical character recognition, or OCR, was a critical factor for allowing the use of digitized primary sources to proliferate. OCR made large bodies of historic documents accessible in new ways, ensuring that these large collections of text would become more discoverable than non-digitized ones.[40] One could now keyword-search across hundreds of years and thousands of pages. OCR arose in a context of needing to make sense of large bodies of documents, such as in corporate legal discovery. Enterprising individuals realized that this technology could be used in other domains such as searching decades of historical newspapers. Throughout the 1990s, pilot projects were carried out (at Yale and Cornell) which explored the scanning of microfilm.[41] In 1999, however, R. J. (Bob) Huggins saw a business opportunity in scanning digitized newspapers.

Huggins, a Canadian entrepreneur, founded his company Cold North Wind to scan entire microfilm reels, run them through the OCR process, create a searchable full-text index, and make them accessible to fees-paying customers.[42] In 1999, high-speed internet access was not widespread, a precondition for sending larger images between locations. Huggins, however, anticipated the widespread revolution in high-speed internet access in the developed world and thus came online at just the right time. Thanks to this, the *Toronto Star* apparently became the first fully searchable and accessible digitized newspaper in the world.

Compared to Project Gutenberg's earlier volunteer efforts, or even the digitization efforts of pioneering digital scholars and library-based digitization projects, Cold North Wind adopted a different approach. It represented a shift away from internal teams digitizing material themselves towards external vendors doing the work for them. If the roots of mass digitization had been laid in volunteer projects like Project Gutenberg or scholarly grant-funded activities, the story would have been different (engaging in hypotheticals: digitized holdings would be more accessible but rarer). Similarly, the use of OCR meant that high-resolution images were necessary, as the unreliability of

---

[40] Cohen and Rosenzweig, *Digital History*, ch. 4.

[41] Chapman, Conway, and Kenney, *Digital Imaging and Preservation Microfilm*.

[42] This paragraph draws on the short history at https://paperofrecord.hypernet.ca/default.asp.

automated transcription meant scholars needed to look at the original and not just a text representation. This made high-speed Internet essential for access, exacerbating an internet access divide between Global North and South as well as between well-served urban areas and the less-connected rural. Finally, as noted, the use of microfilm as the foundation of these projects is also significant. Given that certain material was microfilmed over other material, reflecting both the scholarly interests of past generations as well as commercial imperatives, these earlier biases were written into contemporary databases.

Furthermore, access to massive repositories soon facilitated scholarship but led to a patchwork of vendors (ProQuest digitizing *these* resources, Gale a *different* set of documents). Silos formed, antithetical to the broad approaches that historians tend to take with sources. It also made digitized culture especially vulnerable. While independent companies like Cold North Wind were a boon for scholarship, commercial success was elusive. Huggins was not alone in facing difficulties around sustainability and monetizing access to digitized culture: Google also shuttered its Google News Archive in 2011 after only three years. One exception to this has been the increasing role played by genealogy companies such as ancestry.com in digitization. Moving beyond census rolls to newspapers, in 2012 ancestry.com spun off newspapers.com, providing access to millions of digitized articles. While their core business may have originally been genealogists looking for birth and death notices, the OCR layer opened up hundreds of periodicals to researchers. Over at ancestry.com itself, a large array of material is digitized, moving beyond traditional census data to information such as ship and prison registries.

It all comes at a cost, however. To safeguard their intellectual property and investment, these growing bodies of digitized sources would be hidden behind legally enforced password-protected paywalls. What would be a minor frustration for institutionally backed scholars became a major barrier to those without institutional affiliation. External library borrowing status often did not include access to large and expensive databases, exacerbating the divide between richer and poorer universities. Microfilm had been a one-time purchase, open to all who could physically attend the library. In other words, the consumption of historical sources is now closer to a streaming model (think Netflix or Spotify) rather than a one-time purchase (like a DVD or music album). These databases brought ongoing subscription fees and additional barriers such as the necessity to have a high-speed internet connection.

Indeed, sites like ancestry.com or newspapers.com are somewhat democratic in that they allow individual researchers to subscribe. This makes them access-ible in a way that the large publishing organizations and their institutional focus are not. Yet in some cases, the genealogical use case can collide with the historical one. The UK-based company Find My Past, for example, digitized the 1921 UK Census with The National Archives. They charge $4.90 USD for each image and $3.50 USD for each page transcript.[43] This works for a user seeking a few relatives, but is unusable for any historical research of a larger scope.

The other factor which led to a dramatic increase in digitization was the advent of cheaper digital photography. While early digitization projects – such as *Valley of the Shadow* or *Who Built America?* – digitized (and in many cases transcribed) documents for broad use, most digital photographs taken of historical sources would soon become proxies for photocopies and disappear into private research collections.

In both respects, the ramping up of digitization which slowly began in the early 2000s would accelerate by the end of that decade as search engine behemoths contemplated what they would gain by having print material appear alongside born-digital results in search engines. Companies felt that it would enhance their search engines, help increase their user share, and have a 'wow' factor as well.[44] Soon there were three book digitization and search coalitions – one led by Google, another by Microsoft, and a third by Yahoo! While Google emerged victorious, with the other projects being abandoned by their corporate partners (the Microsoft-led Open Content Alliance lives on in the Internet Archive's Open Library project), the forty million Google Books titles represent a vision of what mass digitization could make possible.

There are three components of Google Books that have influenced how historians work: snippet search, Culturomics, and HathiTrust. The ability to search across forty million titles using 'snippet' search, when the book is under copyright but a few lines around a keyword result can be shown in many cases, facilitates fact-checking and snap decisions on whether a book is worth exploring in full.[45] Additionally, works not in copyright can be downloaded in their entirety in several formats including PDF and ePUB. Secondly, the high-profile Culturomics project, launched in 2010 to fanfare, provides relative word frequency popularity over centuries of a substantial subset of the Google Books corpus and has increasingly become a staple of conference presentations and scholarship.[46] Thirdly, HathiTrust emerged out of Google Books scans and illustrates the potential of a fully featured digital library.

Sitting in the Global North, of course, means that it can sometimes seem as if barriers to access have been uniformly lowered. Yet while Huggins had

---

[43] See www.findmypast.co.uk/1921-census.

[44] See for example Kelly, 'Scan This Book!'; Hogge, 'Egghead Who Hopes'; Hafner, 'Yahoo Will Scan Books'.

[45] Rutner and Schonfeld, 'Supporting the Changing Research Practices of Historians', 18.

[46] Michel et al., 'Quantitative Analysis'.

correctly predicted broadband access revolutionizing database access for North American academics, much of the world still lacks connections necessary to access these resources. Ever-growing technological requirements, from up-to-date software licenses to cutting-edge hardware, add to these barriers. The minimal computing ethos, driven by a pioneering group of digital humanists, aims to ask us to think of 'computing done under some set of significant constraints of hardware, software, education, network capacity, power, or other factors', with implications for increased access, less environmental impact, and ultimately for the development of more impactful digital projects.[47] All platform designers could benefit from this approach.

2.3 The Implications of Digitization: What's In and What's Out

The sheer amount of digitized materials, however, obscures the reality that not everything is digitized. Most of it is not. Digitization is a resource-intensive process, both in terms of the scanning process and also in describing and making resources discoverable. Undescribed and thus inaccessible data are nearly useless. There are also considerable costs to preserving data in perpetuity. Accordingly, any user of digitized resources needs to ask: what has been digitized? What has not?

What is digitized? The holdings of well-funded institutions, from the Global North, are overrepresented. Even affluent institutions must make hard choices about what to process, balancing user interests and institutional priorities.[48] Digitization thus proceeds unevenly and tends to favour richer countries and more popular collections. Conversely, specialist collections in less-resourced institutions tend not to be digitized. As archives aim to enhance the discoverability of their collections, they are integrated into search engines. Sources appear in Google results, and are cited in Wikipedia articles, with ripple effects on visibility. Critical reflection is necessary when thinking about things that are not digitized.

A 2013 exploration of these questions made a case study of Canadian newspapers and how relatively often they appeared in dissertations on Canadian historical topics between 1997 and 2010. The goal was to measure if a given newspaper's usage increased after being digitized, and whether newspapers that were undigitized were conversely mentioned less. The findings were stark. In 1998, a pre-digitization year with 67 dissertations, the *Toronto Star* appeared 74 times. In 2010, once the paper was online, it appeared 753 times across 69 dissertations. Controlling for sample size, this was a 991 per cent increase. Similar trends were found with the *Globe and Mail*,

---

[47] 'What is Minimal Computing?'.   [48] Mills, 'User Impact'.

another paper that was digitized early. However, the non-digitized *Montreal Gazette* and *Toronto Telegram* decreased by 16 per cent and 72 per cent respectively.[49] This was the 'Matthew Effect' of digitized resources in action: the rich (digitized) got richer in terms of use, whereas the poor (un-digitized) got poorer. It was clear that Huggins' and Cold North Wind's digitization efforts had substantially reworked the ways in which Canadian historians carried out their research. Given the discoverability issues attendant with early-2000s OCR (a word accuracy rate of below 90 per cent was likely), historians were using tools they did not really understand and allowing it to reshape their scholarship.[50]

Historian Tim Hitchcock made a similar but broader point in 2013. He argued that historical work was being transformed without accompanying reflection:

> [A]cademic historians have yet to effectively address the implications of the online and the digital for their scholarship, or to rise to the challenge that these resources present. We need to know about OCR and metadata, and we certainly need to learn how to use the tools of data-mining, GIS and corpus linguistics; and we need to be able to wield the tools of large-scale visualization, as spearheaded by the hard sciences, network theory and 'big data' analysis of the sort implemented in the Google Ngram viewer.[51]

As Hitchcock noted, the forces that we are seeing in the use of digitized newspapers are present in other places, such as Google Books views.

Finally, the uneven landscape of digitization is also influenced by copyright law and policy. The United States is a global behemoth with long (and occasionally growing) copyright terms.[52] There, 96 years must elapse between the publication or release of a film, book, or other copyrighted work before it enters the public domain. This profoundly impacts what is available in open repositories. Public-domain work can quickly proliferate across the Internet Archive and other repositories, whereas copyrighted material is secured behind controlled digital lending walls, paywalls, or is just plain accessible. Just as a digitized newspaper is more citable, material in the public domain is also more discoverable and thus more citable. We perhaps see this effect in citation patterns, where there is some (but not overwhelming) evidence that open-access papers receive more citations.[53] In other words, historians need to understand mediating forces. This becomes more apparent as we dig into the details of digital objects themselves.

[49] Milligan, 'Illusionary Order'. [50] Milligan, 'Illusionary Order'.
[51] Hitchcock, 'Confronting the Digital', 20.
[52] Johns, *Piracy*; Aufderheide and Jaszi, *Reclaiming Fair Use*.
[53] This is a surprisingly robust area of discussion – it appears relatively clear that open-access publications in many subfields receive more citations; however, there are arguments that higher-quality papers may tend to pursue open-access. See Clements, 'Open Access Articles'; Gaule and Maystre, 'Getting Cited'.

2.4 The Text Layer

With the overall contours of what has been digitized (and what has not) having been established, the next question is how historical documents go from being primary sources to being put into a database and made discoverable by keyword search. This question also has significant impact on historical research.

There are several ways that primary sources are made accessible for full-text search. First, they can be manually transcribed by a human – this works well for typewritten as well as handwritten documents, although it naturally cannot scale as easily due to resource limitations. There are only so many words a person can type in a day, and it is monotonous, detail-oriented work. In some cases, this has taken the shape of volunteers transcribing items they deeply care about. With Project Gutenberg, individuals selected books that were of personal interest and transcribed them. Starting in 2000, Gutenberg added an additional layer of crowdsourced proofreaders.[54] Volunteers are finite and are more inclined to pursue projects of personal interest.[55] More recently, a second form of volunteer labour has arisen: crowdsourcing. This is most successful in the case of corpora that might be most useful to a community if it has been made fully searchable in its entirety. For example, census records or immigration files benefit the genealogical community writ large if made accessible. Crowdsourcing has also enabled large-scale translation projects. For example, volunteers are translating over 70,000 French-language articles found within the Enlightenment *Encyclopédie* into English (in an interesting point of continuity, the original *Encyclopédie* was itself collaboratively written by over 140 different authors).[56]

Yet crowdsourcing brings ethical concerns such as whether it is fair to create large corpora without paying people for their time, and it skews towards volunteer interests.[57] Finally, a project can pay for transcripts. If done property, a project can create an impeccable resource. The Old Bailey database, a repository of nearly 200,000 English court cases, used 'double-entry rekeying' to create part of its corpus. Two typists type, and if they diverge, a third individual comes in to resolve the conflict.[58] This process creates nearly flawless transcriptions, but at high cost.

Alternatively, as we have seen in newspaper digitization, projects can turn to algorithms such as OCR. OCR, developed in the late 1970s and continuously refined, has a wide array of applications, from reading license plates to processing thousands of pages of corporate documents. Cold North Wind's application

---

[54] Lebert, *Project Gutenberg*.   [55] Vreede et al., 'Theoretical Model'.
[56] 'About this Project'.   [57] Terras, 'Crowdsourcing'.
[58] Hitchcock and Turkel, 'Old Bailey Proceedings'. It is worth noting that Crymble has found several errors in this corpus, prompting him to wonder if corners were cut in the Old Bailey's transcription. See Crymble, *Technology and the Historian*, 35–6.

of OCR to historical newspapers was only the beginning of a process which would see these algorithms applied to historical books, microfilm reels of vast arrays of documents, and beyond. Today, OCR is an active area of vibrant research throughout the digital libraries and information retrieval communities. While accuracy has improved, at the scale deployed in historical repositories, even a few infrequent character-level errors (a 'n' being misidentified as an 'm' for example) has dramatic impact. Simon Tanner has outlined what a seemingly exceptional 98 per cent success rate really means. This is a reasonable if optimistic figure when working with microfilm:

> For example: [take] a page of 500 words with 2,500 characters. If the OCR engine gives a result of 98% accuracy this equals 50 characters incorrect. However, looked at in word terms this could convert to 50 words incorrect (one character per word) and thus in word accuracy terms would equal 90% accuracy. If 25 words are inaccurate (2 characters on average per word) then this gives 95% in word accuracy terms. If 10 words were inaccurate (average of 5 characters per word) then the word accuracy is 98%.[59]

While some platforms allow for users to correct OCR errors that they find (such as the National Library of Australia's Trove platform), most repositories do not allow you to make corrections, or to even see the underlying raw text that is being searched.[60] OCR mediates text, adding an interpretive layer. In Figure 2, we can see an example of 'good' OCR – with high accuracy; in Figure 3, we can see an example of 'bad' OCR, where the algorithm has been confused by noise in the scan and tight, early twentieth-century periodical columns.

As in so many computational domains, machine learning – a form of artificial intelligence – suggests new approaches for automated text recognition. This promises the expansion of keyword search into historical domains previously imagined beyond its scope, such as the Medieval and Middle Ages. The Transkribus project shows how machine learning can help computers parse handwriting, previously largely beyond OCR's scope due to its lack of standardization. A scholar 'trains' Transkribus to understand the writing of a particular scribe or author's handwriting. In this way Transkribus learns how, for example, one author writes the letter 'a' versus the letter 'b', as opposed to how another author might handwrite those characters.[61] After several hundred pages of teaching Transkribus how to read handwriting, a 'Handwritten Text Recognition' model is trained and can be used on future

---

[59] Tanner, 'Deciding Whether Optical Character Recognition Is Feasible'.

[60] See the details on Trove at https://trove.nla.gov.au/help/become-voluntrove/text-correction.

[61] Colutto et al., 'Transkribus'. My thanks to my PhD student Rebecca MacAlpine who uses Transkribus in her ground-breaking dissertation and has shown me its potential.

ES

The Economist

FOUNDED 1843

NOVEMBER 20, 1954 ONE SHILLING

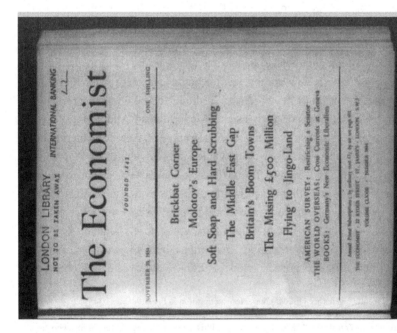

Figure 2 An example of high-quality, successful OCR from the Internet Archive

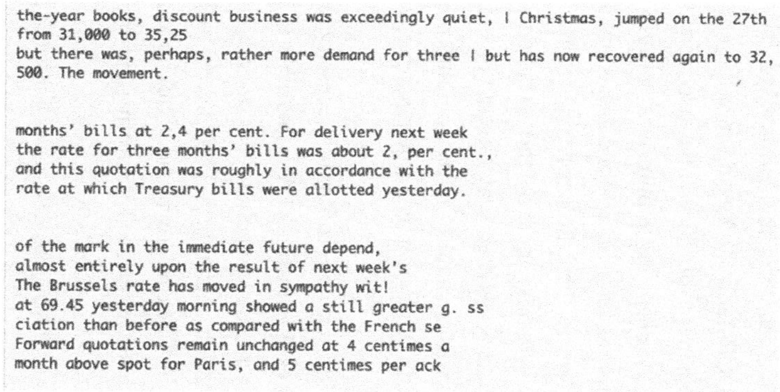

the-year books, discount business was exceedingly quiet, | Christmas, jumped on the 27th
from 31,000 to 35,25
but there was, perhaps, rather more demand for three | but has now recovered again to 32,
500. The movement.

months' bills at 2,4 per cent. For delivery next week
the rate for three months' bills was about 2, per cent.,
and this quotation was roughly in accordance with the
rate at which Treasury bills were allotted yesterday.

of the mark in the immediate future depend,
almost entirely upon the result of next week's
The Brussels rate has moved in sympathy wit!
at 69.45 yesterday morning showed a still greater g. ss
ciation than before as compared with the French se
Forward quotations remain unchanged at 4 centimes a
month above spot for Paris, and 5 centimes per ack

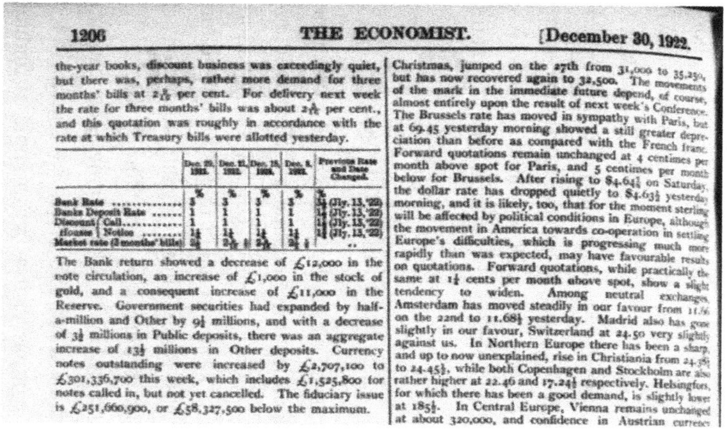

1206 THE ECONOMIST. [December 30, 1922.

the-year books, discount business was exceedingly quiet, but there was, perhaps, rather more demand for three months' bills at $2\frac{3}{16}$ per cent. For delivery next week the rate for three months' bills was about $2\frac{3}{16}$ per cent., and this quotation was roughly in accordance with the rate at which Treasury bills were allotted yesterday.

	Dec. 29, 1922.	Dec. 22, 1922.	Dec. 15, 1922.	Dec. 8, 1922.	Previous Rate and Date Changed.
	%	%	%	%	%
Bank Rate	3	3	3	3	$3\frac{1}{2}$ (Jly. 13, '22)
Banks Deposit Rate	1	1	1	1	$1\frac{1}{2}$ (Jly. 13, '22)
Discount Houses: Call	1	1	1	1	$1\frac{1}{2}$ (Jly. 13, '22)
Discount Houses: Notice	$1\frac{1}{4}$	$1\frac{1}{4}$	$1\frac{1}{4}$	$1\frac{1}{4}$	$1\frac{3}{4}$ (Jly. 13, '22)
Market rate (3 months' bills)	[illegible]	[illegible]	[illegible]	[illegible]	..

The Bank return showed a decrease of £12,000 in the note circulation, an increase of £1,000 in the stock of gold, and a consequent increase of £11,000 in the Reserve. Government securities had expanded by half-a-million and Other by $9\frac{1}{2}$ millions, and with a decrease of $3\frac{1}{2}$ millions in Public deposits, there was an aggregate increase of $13\frac{1}{2}$ millions in Other deposits. Currency notes outstanding were increased by £2,707,100 to £301,336,700 this week, which includes £1,525,800 for notes called in, but not yet cancelled. The fiduciary issue is £251,660,900, or £58,327,500 below the maximum.

Christmas, jumped on the 27th from 31,000 to 35,250, but has now recovered again to 32,500. The movements of the mark in the immediate future depend, of course, almost entirely upon the result of next week's Conference. The Brussels rate has moved in sympathy with Paris, but at 69.45 yesterday morning showed a still greater depreciation than before as compared with the French franc. Forward quotations remain unchanged at 4 centimes per month above spot for Paris, and 5 centimes per month below for Brussels. After rising to $4.64¼ on Saturday, the dollar rate has dropped quietly to $4.63½ yesterday morning, and it is likely, too, that for the moment sterling will be affected by political conditions in Europe, although the movement in America towards co-operation in settling Europe's difficulties, which is progressing much more rapidly than was expected, may have favourable results on quotations. Forward quotations, while practically the same at 1¼ cents per month above spot, show a slight tendency to widen. Among neutral exchanges, Amsterdam has moved steadily in our favour from 11.6 on the 22nd to 11.68½ yesterday. Madrid also has gone slightly in our favour, Switzerland at 24.50 very slightly against us. In Northern Europe there has been a sharp, and up to now unexplained, rise in Christiania from 24.3 to 24.45½, while both Copenhagen and Stockholm are also rather higher at 22.46 and 17.24½ respectively. Helsingfors, for which there has been a good demand, is slightly lower at 185½. In Central Europe, Vienna remains unchanged at about 320,000, and confidence in Austrian currency

Figure 3 An example of lower-quality OCR from the Internet Archive pages. This technology is already being put to fruitful use. For example, a team has trained Transkribus to recognize Michel Foucault's handwriting and is now creating a searchable repository of his profligate handwritten corpora.[62]

Understanding how the text layer is constructed is thus critical for a scholar to understand how to thoughtfully use a database. Is it double-entry text? In theory, it will be nearly 100 per cent accurate. OCR from the 1990s? A scholar will need to do more contextual skimming. Unfortunately, the platform layer often inhibits this.

2.5 The Platform Layer

While some interfaces, such as the Internet Archive, promote skimming and context when exploring collections, most do not. Slow loading times, page-by-page PDF downloads, and results lists all convey that a platform is designed to be primarily searched via keyword rather than systemic skimming or reading. This approach brings risks as the following example demonstrates.

In August 1938, American President Franklin D. Roosevelt visited Queen's University in Canada and gave a speech pledging American support for Canada should the country be threatened.[63] In 2021, I was giving a lecture at Queen's and wanted to use his campus visit as an example of finding information in newspaper databases. To my surprise, a search for 'Kingston' and 'Roosevelt' in 1938 led to *no* results in a search of the *Toronto Star*. Was Roosevelt's visit not significant? Was the OCR faulty? Digging into the newspaper, hosted on ProQuest Historical Newspapers, produced the discovery that there were *no* results from August 1938; indeed, the month was entirely missing. Was this a result of late Depression-era austerity, a publication stop? It seemed unlikely, as in early September letters to the editor referred to articles published only a week before. This was worrisome as it was the first event that I had searched for. If a user just keyword-searches their way through this historical collection, they would not know what was missing. A user could interpret the lack of hits as a null response. They would think of it as a true negative, whereas it might be a false one.

Perhaps, as we used to do with microfilm by necessity, we should return to skimming? ProQuest makes this difficult. A user needs to load a page of the newspaper (via drop-down menus, selecting year, month, and then year). The resolution is too low to read, meaning a PDF needs to be downloaded or manipulated in the browser. Click to download. Click to zoom. Read. Click to the next page. Wait for it to load. And so forth (and then, frustratingly in

---

[62] Massot, Sforzini, and Ventresque, 'Transcribing Foucault's Handwriting'.
[63] 'FDR's Historic Campus Visit'.

ProQuest, when you need to select the next issue, you sometimes need *again* to select year, month, and date). ProQuest is designed for keyword search, with the interface compelling you to access data in that manner. Yet the keyword search is a black box. There is no indication of OCR quality or missing data.

These problems are present in non-profit environments as well, mostly due to copyright. Consider HathiTrust, a repository of digitized books and primary sources. Throughout COVID-19, HathiTrust gained recognition for its Emergency Temporary Access Service (ETAS) which allowed member research libraries to allow their borrowers access to digitized books which they themselves had in their (temporarily inaccessible due to campus closures) physical holdings.[64] This was an essential service for scholars who could now read digitally what they could not physically access. In doing so, however, they confronted the reality that skimming on HathiTrust was different than reading a print book. For copyrighted content, there was no download to PDF option. A user again faced load times, albeit far quicker than ProQuest. For slower, line-by-line readers, the interface worked, as it did for those doing keyword searches (although the text layer was again a black box in copyrighted works). Yet skimming was difficult. Researchers were compelled to keyword-search on large bodies of OCRed text, primarily due to copyright. While the interface appears to have improved by the pandemic's waning days, this still underscores the pressures facing platforms that provide access to copyrighted material.

Enter the Internet Archive. Thanks to its emphasis on public domain materials, the Internet Archive has taken an open approach which empowers researchers to engage with documents and books in various ways. The interface is flexible: one can skim in their web browser, or can download documents either as a PDFs, images, or – importantly – plain OCR text (which is useful to see how messy the text layer is). It is a platform that facilitates research in all of its forms and presents a vision of what could be possible absent copyright and profit motive. It illustrates possibilities.

ProQuest, HathiTrust, and Internet Archive cover a spectrum, underscoring the degree to which copyright and platforms shape our approach to accessing knowledge in the digital age. Yet covering several platforms is important as historians usually require information from across many platforms in a single project. They may locally download from one website, access another through a different paywalled platform, and may be drawn to keyword-search a third. Accordingly, an astute understanding of these interfaces and how they shape our research is critical.

---

[64] 'Emergency Temporary Access Service'.

2.6 Digitization's Impact

The impact of digitization on scholarship is hard to measure. Historians are largely opaque about their methods. This is not due to nefarious motives but rather disciplinary norms. Frustratingly, citation practices cite the source *sans* mediating platform.[65] For example, historians cite the newspaper article but not how they accessed it. While archival citation is better, historians still often cite documents as if they were found in person even if they were accessed online (a bane for those who digitize documents and seek to measure impact).

Despite this citational opacity, changing technology and digitization has affected projects and research questions. Students and faculty can carry out previously impossible projects thanks to their ability to reach quickly and inexpensively across oceans and time. At my Canadian university, where we have shorter, one-year long master's degrees, students can carry out thesis projects without physically entering archives, despite needing to base their research in primary sources. Digital photography means that archival trips are quick, surgical strikes.

Despite the unevenness of the digitized source base, however, it has had considerable implication on the kinds of questions that historians can explore. Instead of having to go deep into one or two newspapers, we can go shallow across dozens – bringing the ability to connect disparate points of information together. This has been a boon for genealogists, as they can find traces of an individual across previously disconnected sources. International connections can be quickly drawn as well.[66] New topics of broader scope can now be pursued. For example, one can easily trace the evolution of public sentiment in a dozen newspapers (and, indeed, these are now questions routinely explored by undergraduates in term papers). Yet these newfound powers need to be better paired with interpretive frameworks. Scholars need to think deliberately about where they are searching and which results to draw on, especially as search results can be drowned out by duplicates. They may also lack the understanding of an article's contextual placement within a periodical.

Lara Putnam examined how source digitization enables transnational and global history scholarship. Previously the domain of senior researchers, who had amassed a body of knowledge after a career of scholarship, such sweeping work is now routinely done by any scholar with pertinent research questions. They can quickly use Wikipedia, HathiTrust, Google Books, or other digitized repositories further to investigate an interesting archival discovery. Imagine: a researcher can sit in a New York City archive, find something of interest that happened in Paris, and quickly Google their way to a few (certainly unrepresentative given digitization

---

[65] Hitchcock, 'Confronting the Digital'.   [66] Putnam, 'Transnational and the Text-Searchable'.

bias) sources. Putnam considers these 'side glances' as having dramatic impact. As she notes, the 'impact of such side-glancing – formerly rare, as each glance would have demanded hours or days of effort with no likely return; now quotidian, requiring nanoseconds to search and minutes to read – has been profound'.[67] Ultimately, according to Putnam, while technology 'has exploded the scope and speed of discovery ... our ability to read accurately the sources we find, and evaluate their significance, cannot magically accelerate apace'.[68] In our own fields we know what has been digitized and what has not been, but this level of critical engagement cannot be extended to every field that we incidentally explore on the Internet.

The digital turn is thus transforming scholarship in three respects. The first is geography, as global projects – at least those drawing on repositories in the Global North, given the costs of digitization – are now possible in previously impossible ways. The second is digitization bias, the 'Matthew Effect' of historical sources. The third is the transformation in the way in which sources are *used*, a shift from contextually aware skimming to surgical keyword search. An understanding of these forces can mitigate the negative effects of these changes. These important concepts cannot be left to be magically solved by the next generation of scholars, but rather need to be actively developed. Our current professional apprenticeship model fails to capture technological shifts, revisioning how we train our students.

What sorts of knowledge must historians acquire in order to properly contextualize their use of digitized primary sources? The first is understanding and being aware of algorithmic bias. Scholars, both to be good historians and citizens, need to think critically about the role that search engines play in their work (and life). Why is one website, for example, the first hit on Google (and thus accordingly cited) whereas another is relegated to the ninth page of results (unlikely to be seen)? What has been digitized and how has it been made discoverable? What voices and perspectives are reflected in digitized materials, and which ones are absent? How was a database constructed? In short, on what information is the scholar basing their arguments on?[69]

The second factor historians need to understand is source mediation and context. How a document is mediated matters as much as its content. A newspaper article read in its original form, or in a clipping file, or via microfilm, or via ProQuest keyword search are all mediated differently – and

---

[67] Putnam, 'Transnational and the Text-Searchable', 383–4.

[68] Putnam, 'Transnational and the Text-Searchable', 377.

[69] I introduce students to the broader political and tangible issues around algorithmic bias via Noble, *Algorithms of Oppression*; O'Neill, *Weapons of Math Destruction*. Historical context can be found in O'Shea, *Future Histories*, ch. 4.

that matters. This needs to be built into our citation practices as everyday transparency. At the very least, citing the trails that we follow reveals these decisions and spurs reflection around whether the medium was influencing the way in which historical knowledge was constructed.

Similarly, the role that search engines play in shaping scholarship is significant. As Ted Underwood has noted, this is not just the shifting level of evidence that might be required to sustain a query – it's rather the fact that a researcher already has a thesis when they enter the keywords with which to uncover. As he notes, researcher's 'guesses about search terms may well project contemporary associations and occlude unfamiliar patterns of thought'.[70] This is compounded by the lack of context on search results that historians provide when we cite our findings – these critical dimensions are largely left uncited and not discussed. Was a source a needle in a haystack, or was it chosen to be representative – and from where was it cited? The platform layer needs to be made more visible in historical scholarship. Jo Guldi argues that scholars must adopt a 'critical search' methodology. She notes that '[c]ritical thinking about the words that supply a digital search lends strength and rigor to our research process ... Iterative approaches and multiple tools are essential for controlling for the scholar's own subjectivity in encounters with the archive'.[71] By transparently documenting choices, research is strengthened and made (somewhat) replicable. Finding the right balance between transparency and overwhelming a reader can be difficult. Yet providing context of search results, a sense of the relative prominence of 'hits' within a database, and other relevant information helps make scholarship intelligible. Databases and interfaces may be completely different and unrecognizable in five or ten years, meaning a historian must always write with this future audience in mind.

Finally, historians need deeper and more substantial digital literacy skills. We need to dismiss the misleading cliché of the 'digital native', and realize that these are actual skills that need to be taught.[72] Unlike our general approach to palaeography and language acquisition, often driven by project-specific needs, the ubiquity of search boxes and digitized documents means that such awareness needs to come early in the historical curriculum (or, arguably, in the base liberal arts curriculum of the twenty-first-century university). By recognizing that all scholarship has been transformed by these forces, we can begin to see that digitized history underpins our contemporary profession whether or not we choose to be Digital Historians.

---

[70] Underwood, 'Theorizing Research Practices', 66.   [71] Guldi, 'Critical Search'.
[72] Bennett, Maton, and Kervin, '"Digital Natives" Debate'.

2.7 Conclusion

Digitized sources will continue to dominate and shape the historical profession. As historians get a deeper understanding of this shift, they will hopefully look back on the first quarter of the twenty-first century as an aberrant period of unreflective digital practice. With more training and attention paid to the mediating influence of platforms, historians need to go down a mental checklist and consider the roles of mediation, algorithmic bias, and context both when they write, read, and evaluate scholarship.

This requires an openness to exploring new forms of scholarship, including moving away from narrative-centric books and articles and thinking broadly about the role of argumentation in the digital age. One of the more important historiographical interventions of the last decade was the 'Digital History & Argument White Paper', a collectively written document by a group of twenty-four historians looking at digital scholarship, argumentation, and – most importantly – the role of the discipline. Aimed at digital scholars, many of its central points are essential reading for all historians. Consider:

> A framework for historical argument that gives little space to methods is increasingly untenable for all historians. A gap has opened up between the assumed method of historians – consulting archives or published material to find sources and then using close reading to identify evidence for an argument – and their actual research practice.[73]

We need to be conscious and understand how our publications and arguments come together, not simply in terms of content and argument, but mediation. And, once understood, we need to write about it in our work.

3 Archives and Access

Archival work looms large in the professional identity of a historian. Archives are where many historians work with traces of the past that have been accessioned, catalogued, and described by archivists, and subsequently shape them into historical arguments and scholarship. Surprisingly, however, historians do not tend to engage critically with archives as an *institution* (as opposed to our engagement with a conceptual 'archive', which has been indeed critically discussed and centred over the last decade or two). Indeed, uncritical reflection on the archive can see it implicitly understood as an unfiltered pipeline. History, however, is not simply a reconstructive exercise, nor is it a synonym for the past.[74] In this uncritical conception, the understanding is that an event happens

---

[73] Arguing with Digital History Workshop, 'Digital History and Argument', 12.
[74] For exemplars, see Jenkins, *Rethinking History*; Munslow, *New History*.

in the past, a record is generated, is archived, and is then read and interpreted by the historian.

Reflecting on archives is particularly important as an interdisciplinary gulf between historians and archivists has emerged over the last half-century. Historians need to theorize and recognize the active role played by the archive, which now includes digitization. In this more robust conception of the role of a contemporary archive, we still begin with an event happening in the past. But we then consider the process by which the record came to be: how an archivist selects only a tiny percentage of the scant records given to them by the document creator (who in turn only passes along a fraction), describing them in particular ways, and eventually a small subset is digitized for online consumption. Choices at all stages have dramatic impact. Instead of there just being one intellectual actor (the historian), in this revised conception we see that many of the active decisions come from the archivist and document owner. During the selection process, as well as the generation of finding aids and metadata, as well as the selection of material to be digitized, the archivist is an active intellectual actor as much as the historian who follows in their footsteps.[75] While the role of the archivist has been evolving, their role in shaping historical understandings of the past has not been limited to the modern period. Historian Patrick Geary, for example, has argued that 'what we think we know about the early Middle Ages is largely determined by what people of the early eleventh century wished themselves and their contemporaries to know about the past', meaning that the popular understanding of a 'dark age' may have more to do with record keeping practices than historical fact.[76]

While archival work is continually evolving, the digital age has served as an accelerant to exiting trends. The selection role of the archivist has evolved, as archivists worry about triage by IT professionals as well as the sheer explosion of digital records.[77] Finding aid and metadata also vary in quality, meaning that the relative discoverability of items varies depending on the time and resources put into its generation.

Compounding this are changes that have taken place in how historians engage with archives. While historians have traditionally approached archives by physically visiting reading rooms, consulting documents, taking notes and photocopies, and discovering new tangents to request new archival collections to then explore, this process has also been transformed by digital technology. This traditional approach should not be overly idealized: some historians had to make do with reams of photocopies, which even at twenty-five cents (or more)

---

[75] Cook, 'Archive(s) Is a Foreign Country', 504. [76] Geary, *Phantoms of Remembrance*, 177.

[77] Millar, *Matter of Facts*; Corrado and Moulaison, *Digital Preservation*.

a sheet could be cheaper than working in situ in an archive. Yet there was a real element of place-based research that saw historians working in archives over a period of weeks or months.[78] Historians working on similar topics would discuss their topics with each other, recognizing familiar faces and discussing documents over coffee, building community as they worked. While one should not idealize this – such prolonged archival visits were the preserve of a fortunate cadre of historians – extended *in situ* research served as the ideal state of historical scholarship.

The situation is very different today. Today, almost all historians – in a survey of historians who work in Canada, about 95 per cent of scholars use digital photography in the archives; 90 per cent significantly – research by quickly traveling to archives, taking hundreds or thousands of photographs, and then returning home to read them there.[79] Digital photography has led to the creation of discrete collection and analysis stages. Rabbit holes are harder to follow, often requiring a trip back to the archive rather than submitting a request slip at the reading room desk.[80]

It is important to understand what this archival transformation means for historical research. To do so, we need to explore two questions. First, what are the implications of bifurcated collection and analysis? Secondly, what is the impact of widespread archival digitization? This requires an understanding of what has been digitized and what has not. By doing so, we can understand how these emerging bodies of archival collections can be leveraged to transform scholarship.

3.1 Changing Work in the Archives

Archives have constantly evolved over the last century. In the 1920s, archives were understood through the 'custodialist' model, a gendered vision of archivists as the 'handmaidens' of history.[81] This was an idealistic view of archivists as neutral actors who transmitted documents from the past to the present for analysis.[82] In some ways, this was mirrored the then-prevailing empiricist ethos of academic historians, where a historian was understood as being able to reconstruct the past as it essentially was through hard work and conscientiousness.[83] Yet, just as this objectivism was always a 'noble dream'

---

[78] Milligan, 'We Are All Digital Now'; Putnam, 'Transnational and the Text-Searchable'.
[79] Milligan, 'We Are All Digital Now'.
[80] Often a good relationship with an archivist can lead them to help digitize material on your behalf. Of course, forging good relationships with archivists is difficult with such short archival visits.
[81] Cook, 'Archive(s) is a Foreign Country'.
[82] Blouin and Rosenberg, *Processing the Past*, 38.
[83] Blouin and Rosenberg, *Processing the Past*, 16; Novick, *That Noble Dream*.

for historical research, archivists have always had to make choices about what to collect and what not to.[84]

The 'post-custodialist' archival theory turn of the 1970s explicitly recognized the activist role played by archivists in shaping the historical record. One of the leading theorists of post-custodialism, Wisconsin State Archivist F. Gerald Ham, argued that archives were now in an 'age of abundance' and that archivists needed to thus recognize their agency.[85] The early advent of digital records drove this in part, as did the broader growth of bureaucracies. Unfortunately, while archival theory moved into new directions, historians and archivists underwent a professional divorce. In 1975, for example, the Association of Canadian Archivists emerged from its previous professional home as the Archives Section of the Canadian Historical Association.[86] Archivists were correctly conceptualizing their facilities as sites of active engagement and construction, whereas historians tended to see archives as static places. Even today, as Alexandra Walsham has noted, historians can understand archives 'as neutral and unproblematic reservoirs of historical fact'.[87] This divide forms the context for the transformation of historian's archival work in the digital age.

3.1.1 The Transformation of the Physical Research Process

How have archives changed for historians in the digital age when it comes to the in-person research process? It is important not to reify a mythical 'golden age' of archival research. Historians now spend less time in the archive than they had before, but the 'old model' of *in situ* research had weaknesses, as it excluded those with financial limitations and caregiver responsibilities. As noted, only some (or local) scholars could spend months away at archives. For others, mass photocopying and research assistants offered a solution. And for many more, substantial amounts of archival research were largely unattainable. We will never know how much historical scholarship was never written as a result. Imagine the many historians born a few years too early to benefit from the broad democratization heralded by digital cameras and digitization, forced to scale back or abandon projects.

None of what follows should be read as a lament for what we have lost with the advent of digital technology. Rather, I am arguing that mediation affects historical research. Even things that are good on balance can have negative features or unfortunate side effects. While focusing on the archive in this section, it would be remiss not to note that just as the digital turn has transformed our relationship with the archive, it has also affected place-based

---

[84] Novick, *That Noble Dream.*   [85] Fleckner, 'F. Gerald Ham'.   [86] 'About Us'.
[87] Walsham, 'Social History of the Archive', 9.

research and our understanding of material culture. We can now explore the places we study through Google Maps and can engage with local community groups through email and social media. Some of our relations with a historical topic are deepened, other weakened, but all are transformed.

The first change has been the mass digitization of finding aids. Many finding aids are now digitized, but some are not. Even across the Global North finding aid digitization is uneven. At Library and Archives Canada, for example, some finding aids are only available by request (staff presumably photocopy, scan, and email).[88] Similarly, the National Archives of Ireland warn that while recent accessions are part of their online catalogue, older 'material is not always available online and must be searched using hard copy finding aids or card indices'.[89] Compounding this, early finding aids may have been converted into PDFs. However, if they have no text layer, they are inaccessible to search engines and hard to discover outside of institutional webpages.[90] Internationally, some archives still require in-person visits to access finding aids, such as the National Archives and Records Service of South Africa.

This means that those who Google for sources may be unaware of what they are missing. This is compounded by the fact that as archival research has transitioned to strategic digital photo gathering missions, trip and time planning is especially important. As with the Matthew Effect of newspaper digitization, archives that have better online discoverability get more visitors and citations. These in turn drive more scholars to want to access these collections. Certainly, digitization efforts at archives are designed in part to serve researchers and increase metrics.[91]

Then there is the most dramatic change of them all: archival digital photography.[92] Since 2009, my archival work has largely consisted of a week rapidly taking photographs to be read at home. This is common practice: almost all archival researchers use digital cameras, from handheld iPhones to (if allowed) elaborate systems of camera tripods and remote controls. While cameras have had their place in the archives for decades – Fernand Braudel famously used a film camera to capture thousands of archival photographs a day – digital cameras and storage have made this approach accessible to all historians.[93]

---

[88] For example, finding aids are not immediately available for some of these literary archives. See 'List of Fonds and Collections'.
[89] National Archives of Ireland, 'Using the Reading Room'.
[90] Schlottmann, 'Updating Finding Aids'.   [91] Mills, 'User Impact'.
[92] I am paraphrasing my work in Milligan, 'We Are All Digital Now'.
[93] Parker, 'Braudel's "Mediterranean"', 238.

The shift from historians being prohibited from taking photographs in the archives to almost all historians being permitted to do so occurred within the span of a decade. At Library and Archives Canada, it was only in November 2005 that the Self-Serve Digital Copying Pilot program replaced the need to order reproductions at twenty cents a page. Under that scheme, scholars could take photographs but needed to sign a formal reproduction agreement, keep a roster of their photographs, and do so only under the supervision of reading room security. The pilot program was made permanent in 2007.[94] Some other large memory institutions made this shift even more recently. The British Library, for example, only allowed personal devices in 2015.[95]

In 2019, I put numbers behind anecdote. How many historians were using digital photography and how many photographs were they taking? I surveyed 1,466 Canadian-based historians and from the 253 responses learned that 95 per cent used digital cameras in the archive (3 per cent did not by choice and 2 per cent noted that their archives did not allow cameras). These historians were taking many photos. 40 per cent took more than 2,000 photos in their last major research project. I had not properly calibrated my question: some were undoubtedly taking many more than 2,000. Indeed, if one were to take my 253 respondents and assumed the most conservative outlook (i.e., if a respondent indicated that they took more than 2,000 photos count that as 2,001), these respondents alone took at least a quarter of a million photographs.

A dramatic transformation has taken place that has been unaccompanied by training, support, or much conscious consideration. Seventy per cent of my respondents noted that they used their personal device, which may or may not have been selected for its camera. Notably, 90 per cent of historians noted that they received no training and over half were at least open to the possibility of receiving some. My survey demonstrated an undercurrent of constant anxiety around archival photo practices, from best storage practices, to arrangement, to practical questions around ensuring high-quality snaps. Most of this training happens informally between historians in graduate programs and reading rooms. Formal training would help.

The troubling shift here is the way in which arguably one of the most consequential decisions of a research project – what documents to select and read – happens at the beginning of a project when the historian knows the least about their subject. This has always been the case at first, but pre-digital research saw more expertise developed over time in the archive. Follow-up boxes could be

---

[94] See Library and Archives Canada, 'Self-Serve Digital Copying Pilot Project'.

[95] Austin, 'Self-Service Photography'.

requested. Historians could thus shape their project in connection with the archive. It is more difficult to do this when collection and analysis are bifurcated into discrete stages. With digital photography, this deep expertise develops at home, away from the easy ability to follow tangents in the archive. For historians, collection and analysis work best when connected. An oral historian uses follow-up interviews or correspondence to maintain their relationships with interviewees, and place-based historians make return visits to their communities. Connection with research sources is critical for historical practice.

Underscoring this, one of the survey respondents noted that their use of digital photography was 'haphazard'. They noted that they were following in the steps of a senior doctoral student in their program who had done the 'same thing in the archives a few years before'. To this interviewee, the process was 'fairly random! We'll see if I took the right one when it comes time to write things up'.[96] Indeed, the rhetoric of 'writing results up' harkens to a research model more commonly found in the social sciences or hard sciences, rather than the humanities (history bridges the social sciences and humanities, but most mainstream historical writing tends towards the latter).

As with other changes, these are not necessarily bad. Shorter research trips allow researchers to save money as well as spend more time with their families and on other work obligations. Traveling less during our climate emergency is also a benefit. Having the documentary record at one's fingertips for immediate recall also facilitates fact-checking. Historians can also incidentally collect information that may later prove important. Yet the landscape of historical work has changed without accompanying reflection and training, despite openness to it among historians.

Recognizing two important factors will help historians better to take advantage of digital archival photography. Much of this as usual comes down to context, framing, and explicit recognition that the tools through which we mediate our research matter. First, historians need to explicitly recognize the central role of digital photography in their research. It is now core to the historian's craft. In dissertation proposals, grant proposals, and project plans, historians need to be explicit about how they will photograph documents. What is their estimate of roughly how many photos will be taken? What selection criteria will be used? What photos should be taken? Return trips to follow up on material read at home are essential to budget and need to be understood as crucial parts of the research project.

---

[96] As quoted in Milligan, 'We Are All Digital Now', 610.

Data management of this information also raises new questions. What device will be used? How will one ensure quality assurance on photos, so that there are no disappointing moments of illegibility when they return home to explore them? What is a researcher's personal data management plan to ensure the long-term sustainability and stewardship of photographs? Just as some funding agencies or institutions expect researchers to preserve their research notes, our photographs form an essential part of our historical documentation. Could these photographs be shared with the archive or other researchers? These novel forms of documentation – as opposed to notes or photocopied copies – can be easily shared, presenting opportunities for new forms of peer collaboration. These questions are currently rarely explicitly addressed in the planning process, whereas they need to be dealt with alongside questions of content and historiography. Much of this could be dealt with in training, either in graduate programs or as part of professional development. Granting agencies, or more specifically the historians who peer review applications, can play an important leadership role in this respect.

Secondly, these photographs mean that historians are amassing large private research collections. Could any of this be shared for the collective benefit of historians and archivists? During the COVID pandemic and archival reading room closures, I wondered if historians would find ways to share these millions of photographs? Yet there was no groundswell of energy for this.

There are critical obstacles to sharing archival photographs. The first arises from metadata. Sharing photographs without metadata or description is nearly useless. Research requires an understanding of a document's context. Description, taxonomy, and full citation information are all important and require in some cases specialized archival support and training to make them publicly useful. Secondly, the original order of documents as arranged in archives matters. Researchers taking photographs can be selective at times, ignoring material that is obviously not of use – yet in doing so the integrity of the collection for others is compromised. Thirdly, archives need to demonstrate engagement with collections: random photographs online could divert traffic from reading rooms and archival websites, imperilling their ability to deliver on their mission. Finally, donors may be uncomfortable with the digital delivery of their collections. The original vision of a scholar consulting documents in a reading room is very different than the decontextualized posting of documents on the web.[97] On the archival side, workflows are seldom set up to receive this material – and there is often a reluctance to entrust a core aspect of their profession (making information available) to relatively untrained outsiders

---

[97] Robertson, 'Digitization'.

such as historians. This is not undue gatekeeping: standardized taxonomies and clear metadata are foundational to good digitization programs.

Yet these worthy objections stand against the clear benefits of sharing. We have the potential of saving a great deal of time. Do we really want researchers taking the same photos as countless other researchers? Working in this way could open inaccessible collections.[98] Secondly, Library and Archives Canada is also pioneering a new model with their DigiLab program.[99] Researchers can sign an agreement and receive access to a dedicated digitization workstation. In return they fill out a spreadsheet to generate workable metadata to the copies that they take. Both researcher and Library and Archives Canada benefit from this relationship.

Tropy, a software project from the Centre for History and New Media, helps facilitate both the research use of archival photos and their sharing.[100] Designed to organize photographs into a comprehensive and searchable database, Tropy provides customizable metadata templates. Historians fill out essential citation information, such as fond, box, or file, as well as other relevant fields, to help organize their information. All of this can be exported. In theory, metadata and photographs could then be exported en masse to an archive, helping bridge the gap between researcher and institution. However, this vision has not come to fruition. Yet as a personal research tool, Tropy is invaluable. With Tropy, however, users are forced to think about metadata and its importance when developing their personal research collections – and make their lives easier as they cite, take notes, and later recall the photographs that they assembled.

Another laudable model is the community archival portal. Archivists and historians who work on Indigenous histories grapple with the colonial nature of most archives. Canadian historian Thomas Peace has reflected on this challenge. He has highlighted the number of archives necessary to piece together the life of Louis Vincent Sawatanen, a Wendat school teacher who graduated from Dartmouth College in 1781. The 'promise of the digital archive', for Peace, lies in the 'creation of new archival relationships in order to recover historical interconnections by bringing together material related to people, places, communities, or cultures not envisioned by any single archive's organizational structure'.[101] Peace's observations build on projects such as the Native Northeast Portal, which draws together archival collections related to Indigenous nations whose homelands form what is known today as the

---

[98] In the wake of a presentation I gave on this topic, I had several calls with archivists who noted that they informally were always happy to receive copies of digital photographs that historians took in their archives.

[99] As discussed in Milligan, 'We Are All Digital Now'. See also 'DigiLab'.

[100] See https://tropy.org.   [101] Peace, 'New Methods, New Schools, New Stories', 110.

northeastern United States. The portal allows scholars to explore 'related documents that have been separated either as an inherent function of the purpose they sought to serve . . . or by collecting practices that cared little for maintaining a collection's integrity'.[102]

Crucially, this portal (and others such as the Great Lakes Research Alliance for Aboriginal Arts and Culture) collaboratively works with Indigenous communities themselves, who review their digital heritage to ensure the ethical stewardship of cultural objects. For scholars contesting the original archival order of the colonial archive, bringing these digital documents together in new arrangements preserves documentary context (users can quickly refer and return to the original archive) while also working with Indigenous communities to recentre their voices and narratives. Working with communities to re-order and re-combine archives into community-driven collections also serves to decentre traditional scholarly and historical authority. As the colonial archive is decentred, historians need to develop new approaches to understanding their own authority and role in constructing knowledge.

A final consideration: what does it mean that historians are spending less time in the archives and more time at home, working with historical documents on screens? Could one be a French historian if one only visits the country for a week, frantically taking photographs in a Parisian archive before a return flight? Could someone be a historian of the American Civil War if they have never been to the United States? One might well be uneasy with this. There are limitations in having historians with little contemporary understanding of the places they study, especially as historians increasingly recognize the importance of community-engaged history. We run the risk of exacerbating fraught relationships between historians and the people and groups that they study. In Indigenous history, for example, historians are increasingly expected to spend time in contemporary Indigenous communities. Ongoing relationships and taking the time to be present in these communities is essential, even if the scholar is studying events from hundreds of years ago.

Grappling with this ambiguity requires recalibration of implicit professional norms and a discussion around what is gained through place-based knowledge. Given there is benefit to be gained both from the knowledge of another place and culture, as well as being in proximity to similar scholars in reading rooms, we should make sure to explicitly note the importance of tacit knowledge. This may mean residential fellowships (even if shorter, as the three-to-six-month model hurts those with caregiver responsibilities), or when it comes to grant adjudication, an understanding that quicker is not always better; that more time

---

[102] Peace, 'Rethinking Access to the Past', 223.

in an archive brings intangible benefits beyond photographs taken or documents consulted. By making research processes explicit, we raise the prospect of opening new frontiers of historical research.

3.1.2 The Digitization of Archives: From Collections to Microfilm

The digitization landscape is uneven. Historians saw this firsthand during the COVID-19 pandemic, when reading rooms closed for long periods of time (and when they reopened, they often did so with serious capacity restrictions). Some projects could continue almost unaffected due to digitized archival resources whereas others came to a standstill. There are of course areas that have more information digitized than others, both due to size (fields with less extant material can have more coverage) and politics (the choices we make around what to digitize). Yet most archival resources remain undigitized, a state of affairs that will likely persist.

The main reason for this is the expensive nature of digitization. Digitization might seem as simple as just scanning material. Yet this is only a fraction of the process. Costs largely stem from the same reasons that a collection of random digital photographs are not useful: material needs to be described, preserved, and made accessible in long-term storage. Some collections are more amenable to digitization than others, such as when a donor is hesitant to having their material placed online. Compounding this, archives are often under-resourced. In an environment of tight budgets, adding resources too digitization typically requires cutbacks elsewhere. As a result, not everything can be digitized.[103] What tends to be digitized will be material that reflects user interests and institutional priorities. For example, in 2020, as the death of George Floyd spurred protests and institutional reckonings around the world, many archives committed themselves to in part rectifying past bias and imbalance by focusing on the digitization of Black voices.[104] These decisions also shape the historical record, and indeed recognize the importance of digitization in shaping the conversation (otherwise there would not be done). Indeed, the Native Northeast Portal offers one model forward, as it has deeply considered the ethical and professional implications behind digitization. There is considerable work to be done, however, to rectify past imbalances: a factor which always needs to be top of mind when using digitized resources. Such portals are examples of a broader approach by Digital Historians, Digital Humanists, and

---

[103] Thompson, 'Why Don't Archivists Digitize Everything?'.

[104] For example, Harvard's Houghton Library announced that 'for the 2020–21 academic year, Houghton will pause all digital projects to focus solely on building a digital collection related to Black American history'. See Burgess, 'Digitization Focus'.

librarians to create digital portals or collections. Sometimes erroneously understood as 'digital archives', these web-based projects often aggregate resources
from many different places into one interface.[105]

Complementing traditional digitization, organizations are beginning to digitize and make accessible miles of microfilm reels, opening new opportunities for
research.[106] As early as the first decade of this century, many graduate students
did not have to travel to archives. This was not owing to digital photography or
digitization but rather their good fortune that many archival institutions had
microfilmed many popular record groups. Scholars could place inter-library
loan requests and read the microfilms from their home libraries. This was the
fruit of efforts throughout the 1980s and 1990s to microfilm archival collections
and 'brittle books' for preservation and access.[107] However, many of these reels
have now been scanned en masse and placed online. The reels now have
a second life, albeit just as with periodicals historians must reflect on the impact
of digitization bias. As noted, a document may have been microfilmed because
of its popularity in the 1980s, leading to its digitization today.

This digitized microfilm is in many ways easier to access than the actual
microfilm. The first reason for this is that digital interfaces are easier to use than
the actual microfilm machines. Unlike vendor platforms, many archives facilitate downloading of these digitized microfilms and are easier to use. Not
needing to lock material down due to copyright reasons incidentally often
makes for an easier user experience. Accordingly, OCR and search engines
can be enabled. While one needs to keep in mind the lower success rate of using
OCR on microfilm as opposed to print documents (streaks and other errors
interfere with the algorithm), this is a real boon for scholars as they can easily
skim and search. Notably, it can enable transformative digital scholarship:
running programs to extract images, work with the text en masse, and so
forth. Yet while the vast array of digitized content has in general been a net
positive in aggregate, it has unfortunately unfolded in private silos.

3.2 The Siloing of Knowledge

Responding to the high cost of digitization, huge swaths of cultural heritage
have been effectively privatized. Any professor at a research university will see
this firsthand. A 'free trial' will be announced by a university library, or
a salesperson will email a faculty member, offering them access to a cutting-
edge array of primary documents and vendor-specific platforms through which

---

[105] Theimer, 'Archives in Context'.

[106] See an overview of archival documents on microfilm at 'The National Archives: A Pioneer in
Microfilm'.

[107] Gertz, 'Microfilming for Archives and Manuscripts'.

to analyse them. Yet nothing is free. Costs for these platforms are beyond the reach of individuals, and the goal in many cases is to pressure an institutional library to subscribe to them. Indeed, the faculty member would rarely even know the cost of these platforms. Rather than one-time purchases, these are usually ongoing costs. For example, the Wiley Digital Archives platform has invaluable records such as the British Association for the Advancement of Science, the New York Academy of Science, and the Royal College of physicians (1200–1970).[108] Some of these services are very sophisticated. Gale, another vendor, offers their Digital Scholar Lab to carry out transformative digital scholarship – yet only on material to which a library subscribes.

This has led to a siloing of digital archives, problematic given the needs of scholars. Figure 4 demonstrates this in terms of what a historian wants. Yet, with vendor and platform silos, what historians confront is seen in Figure 5.

Each interface is different, leading to an upfront learning curve. And, of course, this is just digitized sources, as there are of course in-person sources to also explore. We have a landscape of scattered silos. This mitigates against both conventional and digitally enabled scholarship, where vendor agreements end up shaping the resources used. Research questions are shaped by commercial interests, as opposed to fundamental questions. Fortunately, there is one inspiring model to look to: the Internet Archive. While I focus on the Internet Archive given its scale and broad utility, we can understand community-run tools and portals (such as the Native Northeast Portal) as offering similar potential.

The Internet Archive has been creating the largest collection of openly accessible digitized material: books, documents, microfilms, and beyond.

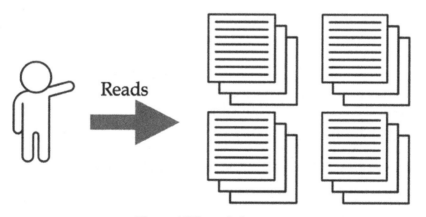

Figure 4 What scholars want

---

[108] 'Wiley Digital Archives', www.wileydigitalarchives.com.

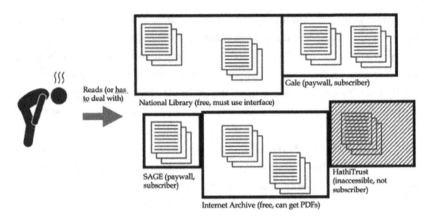

Figure 5 What scholars get

Since its 1996 founding as the Internet's memory bank, it has dramatically expanded in scope and size. In 2004, the Internet Archive began to digitize books – working with libraries to add scanned public domain works to their website – and shortly thereafter in 2005 was part of the founding effort behind the relatively short-lived Open Content Alliance (alongside Yahoo! and several research libraries; it was a public domain and open-access alternative to Google Books).[109] Indeed, today many cultural heritage organizations use the Internet Archive to either freely host their collections, or contract them to physically scan and host their paper materials. In sum, the Internet Archive illustrates what almost-unfettered access to digital culture could look like.

The big-thinking nature of the Internet Archive is worth underscoring. In 2011, for example, Internet Archive founder Brewster Kahle announced his organization's bold vision to digitize *all* of Iceland's heritage and put it online (while evidently this did not get full Icelandic buy-in, a similar project collaborating with the Indonesian province of Bali – via their Bali Cultural Agency – soon followed with more success).[110] Today these efforts proceed thanks to a network of regional digitization centres which digitize material at low cost. Importantly, they look beyond the holdings of affluent research libraries in the Global North (one project is exploring how to build web archiving capacity around the world). With an eye towards copyright, the Internet Archive maintains their Physical Archive in California – owning physical copies allows them

---

[109] Boutin, 'Archivist'; Hafner, 'Yahoo Will Scan Books'; Marcum and Schonfeld, *Along Came Google*.

[110] Kahle, 'Icelandic Literature'; Kahle, 'Balinese Literature'; Widiadana and Erviani, 'Ancient "Lontar" Manuscripts'.

to legally loan them out. The statistics and holdings are impressive: 28 million texts, over six million videos, and 16 million recordings.

Critically, however, the Internet Archive also enables transformative digital scholarship. Documents can be browsed on the screen like a book and can be downloaded as PDFs to work with locally. Raw text can also be accessed directly (and in so doing can allow scholars to gauge the underlying quality of the OCR), and in some cases can even be downloaded as ePUBs. This leads to a flexible workflow: a user can download all the PDFs or plain text in a collection to work with it in the manner that they want. A scholar wanting to read just a few documents might do so on their web browser. In my case, I carried out a recent research project by using the Internet Archive's programming library to download tens of thousands of PDF, text files, PowerPoint files, and images; I could then search it using my operating system's search engine, and stitch them all together to explore much more conveniently than would otherwise have been possible.[111]

The ability to bring all this information together, in a variety of formats, forms an important counterbalance to the uneven digital landscape. It is a portrait of what might be possible absent the silos and barriers that we have thrown up between primary source collections and serves as a worthwhile counterbalance to the uneven digital landscape.

3.3 Conclusion

Given the excitement around the digitization of primary sources, it is important to underscore that most documents will remain undigitized by default. Painstaking archival research will likely always be necessary to some degree due to the varying nature of the historian's craft. Decades from now, one suspects that historians will still be physically traveling to repositories to consult documents. Yet scholars *know* the limitations of the historical record in our area of expertise, making the great undigitized more worrisome when we 'side glance' (per Putnam) to other geographic or temporal domains with which we are less familiar.[112] A scholar taking a peripheral glance at a relatively unfamiliar period or country may not realize the sheer expanse of what has not been digitized in that domain. Their lack of deep knowledge of a field prevents them from being self-reflective about archival silences. This means that whenever we carry out a database search for primary sources we must always ask: what is and is not here?

---

[111] See 'The Internet Archive Python Library', documentation at https://archive.org/services/docs/api/internetarchive/.

[112] Putnam, 'Transnational and the Text-Searchable'.

The way in which historians engage with archives has dramatically transformed over the last two decades. We consult digitized documents from around the world (unevenly due to digitization bias), and we go to archives and take thousands of photos to study at home. Significantly, we allow research to be mediated and shaped by platforms that impact how we answer and explain historical questions. Technology shapes the way we approach our research process, leading to bifurcated collection and analysis stages. This will accelerate over the coming years, as handwritten text recognition begins to make non-typewritten documents discoverable at scale. This acceleration will proceed unevenly, as contemporary issues and policies shape the record. To rise to these new challenges, we need explicit theorization and training. We will also need new publishing models to share our increasingly digital findings.

4 Publishing in the Digital Age

Historians, especially but not only those working in the public history subfield, have a long track record of using new technology to disseminate historical knowledge.[113] Historical work is published not only in books and articles, the traditional career publishing milestones, but also databases, online exhibits, new media projects, blogs, and other platforms such as Wikipedia.

Yet such engagement has been unevenly adopted. Part of this is due to the North American system of tenure and promotion, which takes books and selective journal articles to be the hallmarks of scholarly productivity. This is not due to administrative fiat but rather the need to garner enthusiastic endorsement from external letter writers who may affirm the disciplinary norms of a book for tenure and promotion. There are related concerns with the United Kingdom's Research Excellence Framework. Historians can profess a helplessness in the face of this focus on books and peer-reviewed articles, yet as a self-regulating profession we are our own worst enemies.

Historical publishing is being transformed by digital technology. We can see examples of this in several new and emerging venues. First, some historians are sharing their findings and results through open notebooks and blogs.[114] While individual scholarly blogging has declined, group blogs such as Europeana's engaging blog on European history topics, the generalist Canadian history blog ActiveHistory.ca, or the nursing history-focused

---

[113] Leon, 'Complicating a "Great Man" Narrative'; Robertson, 'Differences between Digital Humanities and Digital History'; Crymble, *Technology and the Historian*.

[114] See, for example, Pulitzer Prize-winning historian Caleb McDaniel's 'Open Notebook History'.

Nursing Clio, form an important outlet for established and emerging scholars alike.[115] Second, in part owing to the decline of formal blogging, many historians are turning to social media platforms such as Twitter or the digital newsletter platform Substack. These range from historians with mega-followings such as Heather Cox Richardson's 'Letters from an American' (the largest Substack newsletter as of 2021) or Princeton historian Kevin Kruse's half-million Twitter followers which have propelled him to national public attention, to the more muted followings of hundreds or thousands for others.[116] Yet it forms an increasingly important venue for historical research and discussion. While not all scholarship needs to speak to the public, these new venues help build connections between historians and a broader audience. Third, responding in part to the pressures of granting agencies, institutional and subject-based repositories – from local institutional repositories to discipline-specific ones such as Humanities Commons – help share pre-prints and other research findings.[117]

These approaches are increasingly a way to make scholarship more accessible by avoiding publisher firewalls. For scholars without institutional access – including those in the global south where subscriptions can be financially out of reach – this is invaluable. Digitization in general has contributed to the time savings discussed earlier in this Element: the days of having to visit the microfilm room to read an old dissertation have passed, giving way to full-text search and discoverability through libraries and other aggregators. This in turn has given way to debates around how long dissertations should be 'embargoed'.[118] All of this means that projects can be shared beyond close peers and conferences as they would have been two decades ago, but increasingly with the public if the author wishes (or, in some cases, does not but has it publicized regardless).[119]

When it comes to traditional outputs such as journal articles or books, traditional publishing has also been transformed. This can involve new developments such as online publishing or open review. It can also be as straightforward as new marketing approaches. While all publishers are different, a recent article published by the present writer led a publication assistant to ask him about social media hashtags, Twitter accounts to target, the option of selective open-access windows paired with a blog post, all with the aim of increasing

---

[115] 'Europeana Blog', www.europeana.eu/en/blog; 'Active History: History Matters', https://activehistory.ca; 'Nursing Clio', https://nursingclio.org. See an overview of scholarly blogging in Crymble, *Technology and the Historian*, 159.

[116] Richardson, 'Letters from an American'; 'Kevin Kruse's Twitter Profile'.

[117] 'Humanities Commons', https://hcommons.org.

[118] Hattem, 'Debating the History Dissertation Embargo'.

[119] See the overview of one interesting case in Grove, 'Naomi Wolf's Dissertation'.

visibility and thus citations. Just as newspapers are cited more frequently if they are digitized, an article might be cited more often if the editorial assistant or author has better social media skills, if the author has dedicated open-access funds, or if a marketing department – as opposed to the academic editor – believes that a blog post or open-access window could bolster the article's visibility.

Even something as seemingly traditional as a 'book' has been transformed. The fact that you are reading this as part of a Cambridge Elements series bears this out. Books are increasingly found in varying lengths and formats, with accompanying datasets hosted on websites and in repositories. Some are even digital-first experiments, presenting arguments in new ways but maintaining the sustained lens and focus of a monograph. As should be familiar by now, these changes are neither inherently good nor bad – but they are transformations needing exploration. In this section, we will explore the changing landscape of historical publishing in the digital age.

4.1 Why Historians Publish

Publishing, broadly defined, lies at the heart of what it means to be a professional historian. This interpretive work defines the discipline. Historians publish for many reasons, none mutually exclusive: a deep commitment to the field, engagement with communities, professional advancement, or (rather rarely inside the academy) monetary gain. Publishing allows a scholar to share knowledge, recover lost stories, reach an audience, and to strengthen their scholarship through critical engagement and conversation. In many cases this means that historians validate and strengthen their scholarship through a process of peer review. These are reasons why historians are drawn to publishers, including academic or trade presses. For the last decade, barriers to online and self-publication have been low enough that almost anybody could just put their own work on the web or self-publish. Yet, most historians realize they are not suited to the task of self-publishing. Self-publishing lacks external quality validation and peer review, necessary for the process of improving one's work.[120] Many authors also look for the professional recognition that comes with a publisher's imprimatur.

Secondarily, historians publish because they are members of a self-governing profession that prizes certain types of publications. In other words, we publish not only in the service of history but also in the service of History. Despite advocacy around the expanding scope of what it means to be a successful

---

[120] Germano, *Getting It Published*, 217.

historian, career milestones remain somewhat narrow and conservative.[121] Publishing operates in a prestige economy, where prestige is associated at least in part with the venue or press itself as opposed to the intrinsic value of the work. In some evaluation contexts, where the work cannot all be read by evaluators, the perceived selectivity of a publishing venue provides a proxy for the value of the work. While prestige and quality may be linked at the macro level – there is some truth to more prestigious venues tending towards more rigorous peer review – this link does not always hold true for individual books. In any event, the prestige of a press is not intrinsic, but rather ascribed by professional peers and networks (indeed, the relative prestige of a press varies dramatically between fields and subfields). Finally, publishers have their own incentives, notably the need for marketability (will a book sell well and recoup costs, or – even rarer – make money).

The complexities of publishing emerge at the nexus of author, profession, and press. Understanding the transformation of historical research in the digital age then requires attention to all three of these factors. An author moving on their own without the validation of professional or press recognition risks muting the impact of their work, but presses and professions rely on individual authors to effect change. All these factors are changing in this new age of digitized history.

4.2 Publishing in the Digital Age

Digital dissemination enables the diverse spread of ideas, using mediums such as blogs, social media, online visualizations and databases, online exhibits, and even innovative digital-first presses which lower bars to innovative scholarship. This has dovetailed with increasing attention being paid to the impact of publicly funded scholarship, such as the United Kingdom's emphasis on 'public impact' in the Research Excellence Framework.[122] Yet this can often exist uneasily alongside disciplinary pressures to focus on traditional books and journal articles.

In Canada, historians have seen the transformative impact of this firsthand thanks to the Social Sciences and Humanities Research Council of Canada (SSHRC) funding agency. While other international funding agencies may have calls for knowledge translation or public impact (such as the National Endowment for the Humanities' Digital Humanities programs, which often stress public engagement), SSHRC now embeds this in all of their funding calls. Historians may still want to publish a monograph as research outputs, but SSHRC's emphasis on diverse and accessible 'knowledge mobilization'

---

[121] Winling, 'Getting Tenure with Digital History'; Tilton, 'On Tenure in Digital History'.

[122] Research Excellence Framework 2021, 'Guidance on Submissions'.

compels scholars to explore new methods of reaching audiences.[123] These are usually digital. Applications are submitted with diverse 'KM' plans that often include blog posts, a podcast, or a website to provide intermediate access to research findings in advance of the monograph. While follow-through is somewhat limited owing to the lack of professional recognition for some of these outputs, it demonstrates the degree to which diverse outputs are increasingly at the core of funder's visions for our (and other) discipline. There is increasing recognition that scholarly outputs should be accessible. Thanks to digital technology, historians are thus actively engaging publics through the web.

4.2.1 Scholarly Blogging

In 2009, a group of doctoral students in a graduate program at York University founded the website ActiveHistory.ca.[124] The idea was that so much of historians' work, informed by great scholarship and research, was inaccessible: overly lengthy, hidden behind paywalls, and written inaccessibly.[125] What if a website could help overcome this?

Our goal was for ActiveHistory.ca to be akin to an open-access online journal which could be a hub for diverse forms of knowledge mobilization: scholars would submit short, accessible, 1,000–3,000-word summaries of their work which would be peer-reviewed and published.[126] Uptake, however, was limited due to the process to which authors were subjected. Going through the peer-review process for a prestigious journal might be worth it, but less so for a website run by graduate students. Onerous revision requests and long turn-around times frustrated contributors, who responded by either not submitting work or by withdrawing work from consideration after the inevitable Reviewer #2 made a pointed request for revision. The editors were arguably asking too much of their authors, lacking both an established audience and more importantly a pedigree to offer in return.

ActiveHistory.ca hit its stride when it turned to scholarly blogging a year later. By 2010, blogging was in its academic heyday. While setting up blogs might seem too daunting for individual scholars, especially those with no technical background, a group blog would help people publish without much investment or experience. They could write their post in a Word document, send it to editors, and it could be edited and published. This worked well: it was a small request (send a few hundred words on your topic) and by abolishing the

---

[123] 'Guidelines for Effective Knowledge Mobilization'.

[124] The group included Thomas Peace, Jim Clifford, Jason Young, Christine McLaughlin, and the present author.

[125] Adcock et al., 'Canadian History Blogging'.

[126] See 'CHA Annual Meeting – Presentation'.

peer review stage and replacing it with light editorial review, there was a lower barrier to acceptance. Authors could write short and responsive 'hot takes' which provided commentary on contemporary issues. They could also use these posts to help publicize other formal, peer-reviewed publications. In an age before Twitter's adoption, this paved the way for ActiveHistory.ca to become a premiere blog for the Canadian historical profession (it was recognized with the Canadian Historical Association's 2016 Public History Prize). The citation noted its impact:

> Activehistory.ca has established itself as a hub of conversation among emerging scholars, senior historians, students, teachers, the media, and other practitioners of public history on a wide range of historical topics. Since 2008, this innovative website has brought historical context and critical commentary to a broad range of political and social issues, and in 2015, it launched many new initiatives, including a digital exhibition page. With 13,000 unique page views per month, Activehistory.ca is committed to making history public and accessible, while setting a high bar for the quality of scholarship it delivers.[127]

ActiveHistory.ca had transformed from traditional publishing to scholarly blogging, serving as a way to understand the ongoing process of digital transformation. Blogging drew on the capabilities of the digital. Rather than trying to make a website conform to the scholarly process (formal submissions, peer review process, author revisions) ActiveHistory.ca embraced the conventions of blogging. This was coincidentally part of the heyday of academic blogging.[128]

As with all transformations, this blogging shift brought good and bad. In the case of ActiveHistory.ca, there was a lot of positive news: the blog garnered large audiences, could be responsive to emerging events, and was open to a wide variety of authors from senior professors to early career researchers to independent scholars. As a web-based medium, it lent itself well to images and embedded digital objects. The group blog format also allowed for editorial improvements and provided a veneer of legitimacy: that is, publication here was not 'just' posting on a personal blog but rather occurred under the curated ActiveHistory.ca imprimatur. This gave authors access to existing social media channels and avoided the stigma that self-publishing may have brought.

There were also disadvantages: the light editing and lack of expert peer review did mean that authors could write things that would not have passed (for good reason) through a peer review process. Similarly, the lack of peer review also meant that few contributors received official credit. This was unpaid

---

[127] See https://cha-shc.ca/english/what-we-do/prizes/public-history-prize.htm.
[128] Crymble, *Technology and the Historian*, ch. 5.

work without formal recognition by the profession, a factor affecting contributors and editors alike. Finally, open comment sections meant that while interesting conversations were fostered, authors – especially early career researchers – were occasionally subject to robust and occasionally harsh discussions. With the rise of Twitter, these conversations moved off moderated comment threads to social media, where they would exist independent of the platform (and thus moderation), in both the formal and informal sense. Yet on reflection, scholarly blogging helped to create robust scholarly commons.

Scholarly blogging declined throughout the 2010s.[129] Institutionally funded platforms such as *The Conversation* – launched in Australia in 2011 but since having spread to international editions for countries and regions including Africa, Canada, Indonesia, the United Kingdom, and the United States – also emerged as a venue for reactive short-form pieces. Yet institutional support meant that *The Conversation* could leverage both professional editors as well as connections to local and national media platforms.[130] Yet, even in an overall context of blogging decline, the group blog model shows that it could be more sustainable in the face of these broader shifts.

Some successful group blogs have even, in light of these pressures or as a result of growing prestige, transformed into websites that increasingly resemble peer-reviewed magazines or journals. *Nursing Clio*, for example, refers to itself as a 'blog project' but in substance and style is an accessible scholarly periodical. They stress their peer review processes.[131] Similarly, the *Black Perspectives* blog has a roster of over fifty regular contributors, and high-quality editing processes. Its homepage looks more like the *Atlantic Monthly*'s homepage than a blog.[132] In some ways, projects like *Nursing Clio* and *Black Perspectives* represent what ActiveHistory.ca originally sought to be. Their path demonstrates the importance of building from a solid 'bloggy' foundation and evolving from there. Yet while these vibrant blogs show the continued relevance of the medium, other historians have turned to publishing via 'micro-blogs' such as Twitter.

4.2.2 The #Twitterstorian

It is hard to generalize about Twitter as it is an ever-changing platform. Indeed, as of writing, Elon Musk had just proposed purchasing the company, which prompted a fraught discussion around the platform's future. Even at the level of the user, Twitter is very different by virtue of with whom a user engages.

---

[129] Crymble, *Technology and the Historian*, 159.   [130] 'Who We Are'.
[131] See https://nursingclio.org for more information.
[132] The blog homepage is at www.aaihs.org/black-perspectives/.

'Academic Twitter' is a different place than 'Young Adult Fiction Twitter' or 'Left Politics Twitter' or, to say the least, something like 'COVID Conspiracy Twitter'. Yet there is no avoiding the reality that as blogs have declined, social media platforms (like Twitter) – have grown in popularity. From historians engaged in historiographical conversations, exchanging ideas about primary sources (such as how to decipher handwriting), it effectively serves as a community hub for the minority of historians actively engaged there. It affords several benefits: low barriers to entry, audiences that can be amplified through retweets or critical engagement, networking opportunities (from forming conference panels to exchanging scholarly sources and publicizing scholarship), commentary on ongoing issues, and threading tweets together to form longform threads more akin to blog posts. Many of these were functions previously occupied by H-Net discussion boards, which have (with notable exceptions) also been somewhat eclipsed first by blogging and now by social media.

The immediacy of Twitter, however, makes for a risky user experience. 'Hot takes' that play well to a small group of historians chatting about an issue can escape that community to be discussed out of context by others. Some historians 'lurk', rarely participating but watching conversations with interest and, again, can miss context that comes with being an active participant. Vitriol can be especially directed at women and minorities, combining the worst of internet culture with academic insensitivity. If Twitter is a water cooler conversation, it is a water cooler on a stage where the audience is hidden by the stage lights. Yet Twitter shapes research: historical scholarship takes place there and is shaped by it.[133]

There are advantages to Twitter engagement and knowledge dissemination: a large audience, the ability to embed media, use of hashtags such as #twitterstorians or #CdnHistory to see related conversations, the immediacy of gatekeeper-less communication, and the ability to forge networks not limited by geography, institution, or field. Historians who are the sole members of their subfield in a department can use Twitter as a venue for regular professional conversations. Live tweeting, while occasionally controversial, opens events beyond their small immediate audiences.[134] Yet there are also disadvantages: the 'outrage' economy of Twitter, a sense of omnipresent surveillance, and the prospect of online harassment. Indeed, the context of 'this is a junior colleague or student, maybe they should be treated gently' can be lost in a sea of

---

[133] This is not the case for other social media platforms. Facebook, in decline as of writing, tends towards the personal. Instagram can sometimes play a role as a public history platform, but short captions and its aversion towards links prevents it from hosting scholarly conversations.

[134] Varin, 'Live-Tweeting at an Academic Conference'.

decontextualized text and avatars.[135] While Twitter plays a complicated role in the historical profession, it is nonetheless a site of considerable importance to the contemporary profession, and worth considering as a historian in the digital age.

4.2.3 Disseminating Research Data

As part of researching a project, historians generate what is broadly defined as research data. In Canada, SSHRC defines such data as 'quantitative social, political and economic data sets; qualitative information in digital format; experimental research data; still and moving image and sound databases; and other digital objects used for analytical purposes', which – generously interpreted – would include a wide variety of data created through historical research.[136] Such data come in many forms: oral history transcripts and recordings, spreadsheets of historical information (such as map coordinates or rosters of people), Digital Humanities-style visualizations, and geospatial data created through Geographical Information System (GIS) software. Perhaps it would even include photographs taken at archives, although this is a bit more complicated due to archival policies, copyright, and the many factors discussed in the previous chapter.

What to do with these data? Traditionally, historians would keep this information private while preparing their book, dissertation, or article. They would then keep it mostly private afterwards. This was partly due to fears around being 'scooped', still a pressing problem today, as well as seeing it as the fruits of 'their' labour. There was also no easy way to share data. In other words, research data in raw form was essentially unpublishable. Even if, for example, oral histories would eventually be deposited at an archive, this would happen only at the end of the project – and in many cases, even interviews would be destroyed after the project's end.[137] The digital age dramatically changed all of this.

These forms of intermediate outputs are now more common, both due to historians increasingly wanting to engage communities as well as firmer direction from granting agencies. SSHRC, for example, mandates that *all* research data be preserved and made sharable:

> All research data collected with the use of SSHRC funds must be preserved and made available for use by others within a reasonable period of time.

---

[135] There are also intentional harassment campaigns. See an overview by Frangou, 'Online Harassment in Academe'.

[136] 'Research Data Archiving Policy'.

[137] This 'destruction by default' has been contested by several scholars, including a team I co-authored with as part of a Royal Society of Canada working group on archiving COVID-19 research. See Jones et al., 'Remembering is a Form of Honouring'.

SSHRC considers 'a reasonable period' to be within two years of the completion of the research project for which the data was collected.[138]

While compliance is not yet systematically tracked or enforced – the policy process in Canada is still under active development – the increasing professional recognition of these deliverables will hopefully shift the conversation. That is not to say that all data must be shared – there is a default colonialist worldview around openness that has been rightfully contested – but that such decisions to share or not share are taken deliberately.[139]

Much of this comes down to the perception of whether something is making a scholarly contribution. Do arranged data make an argument and thus a valuable intervention in scholarly debate? The collaboratively written 2017 'Digital History and Argument' White Paper, published by George Mason University's Centre for History and New Media, explored this, arguing that online databases and visualizations make scholarly arguments and thus need to be recognized as valuable contributions. The examples in the White Paper were wide-ranging, making compelling cases for recognizing the substantive contributions made by outputs such as curated exhibits, datasets, maps, and 3D models. The labour in selection, description, and framing all combine to make these outputs understandable and argumentative scholarly contributions, even if it is not as readily apparent as a thesis-driven book or journal article.[140] Arguably, the decisions we make in constructing a map make it no less an argument than a journal article (just as decisions as part of the archival creation process underscore the crucial role of archivists). Importantly, the White Paper put the onus on author and evaluator alike:

> On the one hand, it aims to demonstrate to the wider historical discipline how digital history is already making arguments in different forms than analog scholarship. On the other hand, it aims to help digital historians weave the scholarship they produce into historiographical conversations in the discipline. The responsibility for integrating digital history with argumentation thus rests both with the digital historians who make implicit or explicit historical arguments and with the rest of the profession who must learn to recognize them.[141]

In other words, the wide range of diverse outputs – datasets, models, maps – were making positive contributions. Common understanding of the labour and thought that goes into datasets and visualizations would help recognize the value of these contributions. Given the importance of professional recognition

---

[138] 'Research Data Archiving Policy'.
[139] See the discussion in Christen, 'Opening Archives'.
[140] Arguing with Digital History Workshop, 'Digital History and Argument'.
[141] Arguing with Digital History Workshop, 'Digital History and Argument'.

and framing for historians' publishing behaviours, this conceptualization is more effective than mandate by fiat. Publishing these data can also help reach new audiences.

An exemplar of a project publishing research data is Cameron Blevins' *Paper Trails: The US Post and the Making of the American West.* It is an example of how research data can be shared when paired with traditional scholarly outputs. Released in 2021 by Oxford University Press, the book was presaged by a variety of publicly accessible digital interventions and accompanied by a digital companion site. Blevins explores the expansion of the American postal network, arguing that the sheer scale of the postal system – almost 60,000 post offices and 400,000 miles of mail routes – requires digital methods to understand. By mapping the 'post on a year-by-year basis', Blevins reveals both the networks' geography and also 'how its machinery worked and the way that it shaped the occupation and incorporation of western territory'.[142] Through data and maps, Blevins illustrates the portrait of what he calls a 'gossamer network', a 'gauzy web, rapidly spinning out new threads to distant locations'.[143]

Importantly, Blevins released the dataset that underpinned the project. Discussed in passing in a 'Note on Methods' at the beginning of *Paper Trails*, his companion dataset is fully downloadable. It is comprehensive, described data – 166,140 post offices between 1639 and 2000 – and the code used to generate it is also available.[144] This data also powers a companion website, 'Gossamer Network', which allows readers to explore interactive versions of maps that support the evidence in the book, or are enhanced versions of figures in the book.[145] Blevins is not alone in sharing data. Historians Kellen Funk and Lincoln Mullen, for example, provided code, underlying programming language packages, and datasets in support of their 2018 *American Historical Review* article 'The Spine of American Law: Digital Text Analysis and U.S. Legal Practice'.[146] Unfortunately, these data-rich historiographical contributions are relatively rare. They are exceptions rather than the norm.

This limited uptake reflects some of the disadvantages to this approach. It is not sufficiently recognized in contemporary professional frameworks. Blevins and his collaborators have clearly done considerable work on these websites, which may or may not be captured by the hiring, tenure, and promotion process (fortunately, Blevins' blockbuster book is recognizable by peers as a marquee

---

[142] Blevins, *Paper Trails*, 5.   [143] Blevins, *Paper Trails*, 9.
[144] Blevins and Helbock, 'US Post Offices'. Helbock, who passed away in 2011, compiled the information; Blevins then took data, cleaned it, and transformed it into a 'spatial-historical dataset'.
[145] Blevins, Wu, and Braun, 'Gossamer Network'.
[146] Funk and Mullen, 'Spine of American Law'.

contribution). Resistance remains within the professional network to understand anything other than a book or peer-reviewed article as a gold standard of research output. Evidence on this is scant, as tenure decisions happen behind closed doors: a departmental chair's unwillingness to engage external reviewers versed in methods and data, for example, as opposed to formal subfields would vary dramatically by institution. However, published tenure-and-promotion guidelines in humanities departments across North American research-intensive universities tend to point towards the necessity of a book for tenure.

While the *American Historical Association* has guidelines for evaluating digital scholarship, they are perhaps a bit short on substance.[147] Yet their existence, coupled with conversations at the AHA annual meetings and in professional publications, give hope for future change. Similarly, the growing acceptance of 'digital dissertations' – unique forms of scholarship that have contested the traditional paper (and now PDF) tome – suggests there is growing openness to change.[148] The profession is currently at the stage of exemplar projects, such as Jeri E. Wieringa's 2019 dissertation.[149]

A related concern is the hesitation to cite datasets. This is both part of the previously discussed tendency to ignore source mediation, as well as an implicit tendency to see data provision as 'service' and not properly constituted research. Finally, sustainability is also a concern. Blevins' data are hosted on GitHub, whereas Kellen and Mullen's are hosted on Oxford University Press's website. Both are relatively safe, long-term choices for storage: but what happens in twenty years if the Press reorganizes its website? Datasets will likely be preserved in multiple places, including by the Internet Archive in its periodic internet crawls. Interactive visualizations have shorter lifespans as underlying software packages sunset and end, and it is more difficult to preserve dynamic web content.

Disadvantages notwithstanding, a transformation is underway. The advantages of this form of scholarship include making historical argument more accessible and understandable by releasing data, thus building a foundation for future scholars, allowing diverse interpretations, and using the technology as intended. Readers can dig into maps themselves, for example, and visualize data as best suits them. Yet there are disadvantages: arguments can be lost; sustainability concerns appear; the lack of recognition; and dataset citation.

---

[147] Digital History Working Group, 'Guidelines'.
[148] See the discussions in Kuhn and Finger, *Shaping the Digital Dissertation*.
[149] Wieringa, 'Modeling the Religious Culture'.

4.3 The Transformation of the Journal and Book

A journal reader might be forgiven for thinking that little has changed in the publishing world. Journal articles continue to be denoted conventionally by volumes, issues, years, and page numbers, and in most but not all cases can be downloaded as typeset PDFs. Sometimes the hyperlinks in these articles work, but not always. Indeed, individual journal articles often do not look dissimilar to those articles published decades earlier. Disciplinary pressures have contributed to this situation. Peer review is essential for the professional recognition of scholarship, typeset PDFs lend credence to publications, and evaluators of CVs often want to see page numbers. Similarly, while open access is an increasing part of the landscape, many journal publications remain closed: limited to institutional subscribers or those who might choose to pay for individual articles. 'Gold' open-access models, requiring authors to pay article processing charges to make a publication available to all readers, are an awkward fit with the modest funding ecosystem available to historians. These pressures are also present in the case of books: publishers take author manuscripts, transform them into typeset documents, and have them bound and published for sale.

Granting agencies, scholarly foundations, scholarly associations, and individual researchers have been spurring a slow transformation of book and journal publishing. MIT Press, for example, now publishes new monographs and edited collections as open access. They are fully downloadable for free, thanks to a combination of support from the Arcadia Fund as well as fees from participating libraries (who receive access to the otherwise closed back catalogue).[150] In 2015, the University of Minnesota Press partnered with the City University of New York's Digital Scholarship Lab to launch the 'Manifold Scholarship' platform. The Manifold platform allows scholars to host rich web-based books – often but not always as a complement to a print book. These rich digital editions facilitate reader interaction with primary sources and images. They allow readers to interact with the author and with each other through in-line annotations and commenting.[151] While the platform has been used by several publishers, the University of Minnesota Press also works with authors to publish iterative drafts of books. These publicly take shape, allowing authors to engage with readers as a draft is written.[152]

Journal and book peer review is also changing. Public participation in open peer review, where drafts are publicly posted and readers invited to comment,

---

[150] See an overview of this policy at https://direct.mit.edu/books/pages/direct-to-open.

[151] See an overview of Manifold at www.upress.umn.edu/press/press-releases/manifold-scholarship.

[152] See an overview of 'Projects in Progress' at https://manifold.umn.edu/projects/project-collection/projects-in-progress.

either informally through in-line comments or annotations or more formally through comprehensive reader reports, aims to produce stronger scholarship through productive open conversations. This process provides diverse perspectives on scholarship, more so than just the two, three, or four standard peer reviewers that evaluate most articles. This model has been around for a while now. In 2014, writing a Digital History textbook alongside my co-authors Shawn Graham and Scott Weingart, we posted the draft of our draft manuscript as sections were written online. These helped build confidence in our textbook – many eyes made for stronger work – although we did note in a retrospective for *Perspectives in History* that it took a bit of a thick skin. It was 'one thing to receive [reviews] quietly in your office when a peer review arrives, but another to undergo the process in public'.[153] Ultimately, our experiment with open review became one of the most rewarding elements of the book.[154]

Recently, even long-established journals have experimented with these new peer review approaches. In 2020, the *American Historical Review* hosted an open review of the article 'History *Can* Be Open Source' by Joseph L. Locke and Ben Wright.[155] The review process combined two evaluation approaches. The journal editor solicited readers who would provide traditional reports and had those publicly posted. The journal also complementarily hosted an open review platform for paragraph-level comments on both the initial as well as the revised manuscript.[156] Anybody could provide feedback on the manuscript. The dozens of comments are testament to an openness towards these new experiments in publishing.

Some recent 'books' are beginning to push at the boundaries of traditional publishing, forcing a rethink of what a 'book' in the digital age might look like. Stanford University Press has emerged as a leader in this space, rethinking digital monographs not just as enriched PDFs or websites but as fully digital publications. Elaine Sullivan's *Constructing the Sacred: Visibility and Ritual Landscape at the Egyptian Necropolis of Saqqara*, winner of the 2020 Roy Rosenzweig Prize for Innovation in Digital History, exemplifies this type of publication. Designed as a digital object first, this argument-driven digital monograph contains videos, high-resolution maps, and even interactive 3D models where you can explore Saqqara, Egypt, and move a timeline slider to explore changes over time. The integral nature of the integrated digital visualizations means that any 'book' version of *Constructing the Sacred* would be a pale imitation.[157]

---

[153] Graham, Milligan, and Weingart, 'Writing the Historian's Macroscope in Public'.

[154] Graham, Milligan, and Weingart, *Exploring Big Historical Data*.

[155] Locke and Wright, 'History Can Be Open Source'.

[156] The open review is hosted at https://ahropenreview.com/HistoryCanBeOpenSource/.

[157] Sullivan, *Constructing the Sacred*.

Journals are also adopting new forms in the digital age. In 2021, the *Journal of Digital History* launched articles which were essentially code-driven 'notebooks'. They combined interactive code snippets and narrative prose. One can interact with a database while reading the article, for example, allowing a user to interact with the primary sources or information on the very same page as the article itself. This approach to 'transmedia storytelling' allows researchers to feature their methodological approaches through a hermeneutical 'layer', resulting in a new form of scholarship. While still a new journal, their first issue contained articles on text mining in newspapers, Twitter mining to understand public commemoration and computational explorations of Tacitus' works.[158]

These new approaches present challenges. Sustainability is first and foremost of these. New forms of dynamic and interactive scholarship require new methods of digital preservation to ensure a book or journal is replayable in a decade or century from now. Workflows designed to preserve print scholarship or static PDFs do not always work with dynamic, interactive projects. At Stanford University Press, a years-long project funded by the Andrew W. Mellon Foundation witnessed a collaboration between the Press, a web archiving project (Webrecorder), and the Stanford Digital Repository to ensure the long-term preservation of digital books. Their project blog underscores the sheer difficulty facing even a very well-resourced team in ensuring the high-fidelity replay of these 'books' in the future.[159]

Past pitfalls illustrate the dangers of adopting digital publishing without sufficient attention to sustainability. In 2003, digital historian Roy Rosenzweig published an *American Historical Review* article entitled 'Scarcity or Abundance?'[160] Simultaneous to its publication, the journal hosted an online discussion forum. While it was promised to form part of the journal record, when the journal moved from the community-supported HistoryCooperative.org site to Oxford University Press, these discussions disappeared and were thus only serendipitously preserved by the Internet Archive.[161]

The final challenges present in all of this as well are the financial challenges: book and journal publishers rely on purchases and subscription fees to recoup expenses (and make a profit in some cases to enable the cross-subsidy of less-commercially successful works). In the case of book publishers, this extends far beyond producing a print object, but include the work that goes into selection,

---

[158] See for example Oberbichler and Pfanzelter, 'Topic-Specific Corpus Building'; Smyth and Echavarria, 'Twitter and Feminist Commemoration'; Autin, 'Nameless Crowds'.

[159] See the project blog at http://blog.supdigital.org/signed-sealed-delivered/.

[160] Rosenzweig, 'Scarcity or Abundance?'.　　[161] Katz, 'Publishing History Digitally'.

peer review, marketing, editorial feedback, and beyond.[162] Open access requires different financial models to succeed. Perhaps the success of the MIT Press open access approach will spur broader sectoral change.

To end this section on a meta point, let me turn to forms of publications such as the one that you are reading: linear publications that take the shape of a book or journal article, but which take advantage of new opportunities presented by digital technology. There are a variety of these kinds of publications. Short monographs such as Cambridge Elements, Palgrave Pivots, Oxford Very Short Introductions, and beyond; 20,000 to 30,000 words, often consumed digitally rather than via print. This is made possible by the digital turn.[163] While open-access publishing in traditional historical venues, such as books and journal articles, is relatively rare due to its cost and smaller grant agency support in the humanities, it is growing (especially in the United Kingdom where funders are increasingly mandating this). Naturally, we are now seeing the rise of digital editions: dynamic digital versions to *complement* (rather than replace, in the case of Stanford University Press digital projects) traditional print versions, although experiences have been uneven.[164]

Challenges aside, it is clear that traditional forms of the 'book' and the 'journal article' are beginning to be reshaped in new and interesting ways. Perhaps this represents a useful pathway forward for the profession. Such scholarship is intelligible to history departments, external evaluators, and deans, but draws on new and emerging technologies. Ultimately, the digital age will perhaps be most visibly demonstrated in the changing ways in which historians publish and share their research.

4.4 Conclusion

We are in a transitional stage of digital publishing: innovations of novel approaches are combined with the linear argumentation and recognizable form of a monograph or article. It can accordingly make a strong professional impact. Indeed, it is this calculus that lies in the Element you are reading: a linear argument in a recognizable form, but accessed and shared online.

Ultimately, the shape of how historians exchange our findings and engage with the public determines what history will look like in the digital age. It is exciting: historians no longer simply need to turn to a handful of presses and venues through which to publish work in the same typeset, linear fashion.

---

[162] Germano, *Getting It Published*, 211.

[163] McCall and Bourke-Waite, 'Academic Book of the Future'.

[164] I was struck by Sheila Brennan's negative experience in this respect. See Brennan, 'My Digital Publishing Update'.

Yet it is also a bit worrying: choice overwhelms, and the variety of mediums means that their reception amongst the public and the profession are uncertain. The final question then is: what can we do to transform the historical profession so that it can meet the challenges of the digital age?

5 Conclusion

The profession of history has undergone dramatic transformation in the digital age – an ongoing process accelerated even further by the COVID pandemic. New and emerging technologies have changed how historians engage with libraries and archives, as scholars increasingly avail themselves of new approaches which allow them quick access to information, such as digital photography or keyword search. Increasingly, archivally focused historians are part of 'a desk discipline' where data collection and data analysis are bifurcated stages. Compounding this, historical work with documents more generally has changed as researchers are drawn towards digitized sources and *away* from contextually aware research. These digitized sources are in turn shaped by algorithms that are rarely seen or understood. Finally, the way in which historians disseminate their findings, from blog posts to books, has also shifted, requiring new approaches to how the profession values and understands scholarship. And these changes continue, with dramatic implications for how we carry out our craft. What should historians do as a professional discipline to respond to these changes?

Our profession needs to transform in four main ways: understanding the importance of digital literacy, recognizing the value of interdisciplinarity, prioritizing methodological discussions and reflections, and finally, changing part of our training process. The challenge of digital sources may at first overwhelm, but several small, incremental tweaks and recognitions can put historians on a more rigorous path. As historians have long understood the value of context, we are well positioned to rise to these challenges.

We need to first recognize the value of digital literacy, something which is necessary not just for historians but also for all scholars. All historians have been transformed by digital technology, whether they are Digital Historians or historians influenced by the digital turn (digital historians). Given the wide array of digitized primary and secondary sources, ultimately all historical sources are mediated to some degree through technology. Even sources still consulted exclusively on paper have been made more easily discoverable by digitized finding aids, or they are contextualized and read within a larger body of digital material. As noted at the beginning of this Element, the genie is out of the bottle. We are not going back to a pre-digital era of scholarship where we eschew the advantages of digital technology, any more than scholars of the early sixteenth century were going to revert to manuscript-only publication. Yet we need to consciously think about the role of the digital. By citing sources as they are mediated – a newspaper from the *Globe and Mail* as found in ProQuest, for example, or via a microfilm reel – can both make historians think consciously about their research methods as well as open opportunities for peer reviewers to push authors to be more self-reflective. Through this, historical methods will be explicitly spelled out rather than left implicit. This in turn can spread to the classroom, as educators encourage students to critically reflect on the mediation and selection of their sources (and as exemplified by the texts they read). This in turn can help make our students more critical and conscious consumers of information.

Accordingly, the ways that we publish and write also need adjustment. Historians too often shy away from explicit methodological discussions, relegating such conversations to footnotes or the scholarly equivalent of the cutting-room floor.[165] Yet if historians want consciously to reflect in our writing on the role of technological mediation, more discussions are needed. Perhaps that can take the shape adopted by Blevins' study of the post office: a note at the front of the book, inviting the reader to explore more in companion material.[166] Or, in journal articles, it could become fundamental to research practice – a recognition that process and mediation are as significant as the finding themselves, given the scale of the repositories we are exploring. While historians enjoy good, engaged writing, scholarly journals are sites of professional, specialist discussion. Surely there is more room for methodological discussion.

The second necessary change is that we need to understand the role played by everyday interdisciplinarity. As we saw earlier, the growing gulf between archives and historians that has emerged since the 1970s means that – as Blouin Jr. and Rosenberg argued – a historian using an archive is engaging in a form of interdisciplinary research.[167] Historians need to embrace this. We should cite archivists, drawing on the development of archival theory which is happening in venues such as *Archivaria* or the *American Archivist*, as well as on an array of scholarly blogs and edited collections. This scholarship explores the way in which archives (digital and traditional alike) are constructed, with profound impact on historical scholarship.[168] This logic extends to other

---

[165] In the *Digital History and Argument* white paper and workshop, there was consensus among the many authors: 'The experience of workshop participants has been that reviewers and editors frequently insist that methodological sections be cut or shortened to avoid disrupting the narrative'. See Arguing with Digital History Workshop, 'Digital History and Argument', 12.

[166] Blevins, *Paper Trails.*   [167] Blouin and Rosenberg, *Processing the Past*, 10.

[168] St. Onge, 'Collaboration'.

platforms and interfaces. When we use a search engine or a database, we are also engaging in a form of interdisciplinarity as the products of other academic fields shape the structure of our knowledge. Why is one result ranked #1 and another #100? What technology was used to transcribe a document? There are robust scholarly literatures on these questions, which can help us open the 'black boxes' that control and shape scholarly research. Interdisciplinary engagement with the library and information studies field can better complicate digitally informed historical work.[169]

The third necessary transformation is a need to privilege methodology more generally. This must extend to how we conceive of, and organize, our profession. In hiring fields and curricula, and even the way we present ourselves on departmental webpages and each other, historians privilege geographic fields and temporal periods. One is a twentieth-Century historian of the United States, a nineteenth-century historian of Canada, or a historian of Postwar Britain, a global historian, and so forth. Even when digital history is a central consideration, job advertisements tend to specify a geographic area as well. Yet the forces discussed in this Element transcend geography and era. Digital technology affects everybody. Methodological discussions also struggle to get onto the content-heavy curricula of courses. While we might see geographic context or period as keys to building a professional foundation, algorithmic or methodological context is equally important. Just as we need to have room for methods sections that do not get cut by editors, we need openness to hiring, tenuring, and teaching by method rather than geography. Part of the solution to this might be the embracing of more interdisciplinary offerings across the curriculum. Considering the common methodological needs of historians, English language and literature, and anthropology, for example, might help broaden curricula and help regenerate our teaching approaches for the twenty-first century.

This leads to the fourth and final factor: the need to change how historians are trained. Required undergraduate methods courses, especially those in digital methods, are rare in North America. Methods courses are not just needed to teach undergraduates about how to become historians, but more importantly, how to become attuned to issues of context, algorithms and beyond that can equip them to be good citizens. Graduate education primarily focuses on content, not craft. In general, historians learn to become professional historians through an apprenticeship model. They learn from their supervisors and committee members how to be rigorous researchers. This approach is generally

---

[169] For an example of this wherein information scholars, a librarian, and a historian collaborated to 'open the black box' of an archival collection. See Maemura et al., 'If These Crawls Could Talk'.

sound, but its emphasis on reproducing past patterns of scholarship and research means that major paradigm and medium shifts can be missed. The role technology has played in historical scholarship has happened so slowly, that it has almost happened invisibly. It is only when looking back over twenty years that we can see how profoundly our research workflows have changed.

Historians need to recognize that they are living through a major change in how historical research is carried out, and accordingly change the way in which they train, write, and think about the past and its mediation. There has been some sporadic discussion of this in the profession: special sections exploring digital methods in flagship journals such as the *American Historical Review*, as well as well-attended conference roundtables at conferences such as the American Historical Association.[170] More needs to be done, however, given that these digital transformations are arguably the defining issue of the profession today.

There are obstacles to these changes. Many of these stem from the hierarchical nature of the historical profession. As a self-regulating profession, senior members make decisions about what will or will not be valued. These include conversations about whether interdisciplinary scholarship belongs in a given journal or conference, to the role of methodological discussions in published scholarship, to the organization of graduate programs. Institutional change comes slowly. Academics need to be engaged in their service and leadership networks, so as to ensure our profession can rise to the challenges before it.

These issues cut across the disciplinary silos of the modern university. All students need an awareness of algorithmic bias, an understanding of how content is mediated and contextualized, and broader digital literacy skills. We do a great deal of implicit leaning on the idea of a 'digital native', which ignores students' uneven technical skills.[171] We all need to engage with these cross-disciplinary problems that are transforming our world.

The potential benefits reach beyond the academy. Indeed, these skills might make a history student better able to understand the provenance of a digital source they are looking at, but they might also make them a citizen better able to understand and parse the plethora of (mis)information they are confronted by daily. Thinking about the context and mediation of a newspaper article from decades-old newspapers develops skills to evaluate the trustworthiness of a tweet or a newspaper article that pops up on Twitter or TikTok. Perhaps this

---

[170] The *American Historical Review* currently has a section 'Writing History in a Digital Age' overseen by consulting editor Lara Putnam; the *Canadian Historical Review* published a 'Forum' on digital scholarship in their December 2020 issue.

[171] Eynon, 'Myth of the Digital Native'; Selwyn, 'Digital Native'.

is ultimately less about making 'good' historians than making us all better consumers of information.

The importance of context has been an important theme throughout this Element. Historical scholarship is often driven by historical documents – from tweets to government paperwork to private correspondence. In all cases, historians seek to understand them in their historical context, including authorship, reception, environment, culture, and period. To this, I would add source mediation and algorithms. As we increasingly rely on digital information, historians, and our grasp of context, will become more important than ever.

Consider the pressing problem of 'deepfakes', fake yet realistic-looking videos manipulated or generated by artificial intelligence. As videos are considered trustworthy, these present a very real challenge to how we understand what we seem to be seeing with our own eyes. These range from viral yet fake videos of movie star Tom Cruise saying and doing odd things such as magic tricks or praising bubble gum, to bringing historical figures to life so that it seems that Abraham Lincoln was captured on video.[172] They portend an increasingly fraught historical record to come. Yet historians have always been experts at parsing misinformation, bias, misrepresentation and beyond in traditional archival repositories (the provenance of material in Library and Archives Canada might be assured, but historians still interpret individual documents there with care). If we read an archival document that surprises us as an expert reader, breaking with our accepted understanding, a good historian does not rashly jump to conclusions. We instead try to contextualize what we have just learned. A historian attuned to historical context should not be hoodwinked by an outlier.

Historians are specialists in critically reading documents and then confirming them. Findings are synthesized and contextualized among a broad array of additional sources and voices. Historians tie together big pictures and findings. The work of a historian might look different in the twenty-first century – exploring databases, parsing digital information – but the application of our fundamental skills of seeking context and accumulating knowledge will serve both society and the historical profession well in the digital age.

Changes are rarely ever simply 'good' or 'bad'. Rather, these transformations require further contextualization and conscious deliberation. In many cases, being self-conscious and self-reflective in the way that we carry out our scholarship ensures that we will better benefit from the resources and approaches that we draw on. Historians are all digital now: they need to embrace

---

[172] Gibson, 'Keeping it Real'.

that reality. There is room for a robust field of Digital History that can use computational technology in new ways to push forward historiographical frontiers, but it cannot be the only site of critical engagement with technology across our profession.

Next time you pick up a digital camera in an archive and take a picture of a document, or search for a document on ProQuest, or tweet about your research, pause and reflect on what you are doing. Ask yourself these questions. Is the platform changing what I am doing? How can I make sure I am controlling my research workflow? A series of critical questions can make us better consumers of information. Similarly, the next time you see a viral tweet prompting you to hesitate to take a vaccine or to panic about something, perhaps you will be better equipped to understand how it is being mediated. If we are all digital, imagine the opportunities that lie ahead.

Glossary

Algorithm: An algorithm refers to a set of instructions or rules that a computer follows to solve a problem.

Blog: While blogs began as 'web diaries' or 'web logs', the explosion of scholarly and popular blogging in the 2000s was facilitated by Content Management Systems that made web publishing accessible. For example, a user could quickly start a WordPress or Blogger site. They could then publish text and images through filling out a web form or dragging-and-dropping graphics.

Internet Archive: Founded in 1996 by entrepreneur Brewster Kahle, the Internet Archive is a San Francisco-based digital library with the mission of 'universal access to all knowledge'. While they were originally dedicated to creating an archive of the World Wide Web, within years they expanded to collect expansive video, audio, and digitized print.

Machine learning: Machine learning is an artificial intelligence approach to teaching a machine how to classify information or make decisions. It does so by exposing a computer to 'training data' to construct a model which can then be applied to new data.

Microfilm: Microfilm is a medium created by taking images, reducing them in size (which varies but often 1/25th size), and then putting images onto microfilm reels or microfiche sheets. These small images can then be reproduced through magnification by using a microfilm reader.

Optical Character Recognition (OCR):   Optical character recognition is the automated process by which an algorithm (see 'Algorithm') transforms an image of text, whether typewritten or handwritten, into computer-readable text. For decades, OCR had been limited to typeset documents. However, advents in artificial intelligence (see 'Machine Learning') have enabled handwritten recognition.

Portable Document Format (PDF):   A PDF is a standardized file format that combines graphics and text. For historians, they are commonly used as a file format to reproduce historical documents.

Substack: Substack is an online newsletter service. Authors can create newsletters for either a free or paid audience. These are primarily delivered through email.

Twitter: Twitter is a 'micro-blogging' service founded in 2006. A user can create a Twitter account and then share their thoughts in short snippets – originally 140 characters, now 280. Users can also share images and other rich media.

Bibliography

'About this Project', *The Encyclopedia of Diderot & d'Alembert*, https://quod .lib.umich.edu/d/did/intro.html.

'About Us', *Association of Canadian Archivist*, https://www.archivists.ca/con tent/about-us.

Adcock, Tina, Keith Grant, Stacy Nation-Knapper, Beth Robertson, and Corey Slumkoski, 'Canadian History Blogging: Reflections at the Intersection of Digital Storytelling, Academic Research, and Public Outreach', *Journal of the Canadian Historical Association*, 27, no. 2 (2016), 1–39.

Anderson, Ian, 'History and Computing', *Making History: The Changing Face of the Profession in Britain*, 2008, https://archives.history.ac.uk/making history/resources/articles/history_and_computing.html.

Arguing with Digital History Workshop, 'Digital History and Argument', *Roy Rosenzweig Center for History and New Media*, 13 November 2017, https:// rrchnm.org/argument-white-paper/.

Armitage, David and Jo Guldi, 'The History Manifesto: A Reply to Deborah Cohen and Peter Mandler', *American Historical Review*, 120, no. 2 (April 2015), 543–54.

Auerbach, Jonathan and Lisa Gitelman, 'Microfilm, Containment, and the Cold War', *American Literary History*, 19, no. 3 (Fall 2007), 745–68.

Aufderheide, Patricia and Peter Jaszi, *Reclaiming Fair Use: How to Put Balance Back in Copyright*, 2nd ed. Chicago: University of Chicago Press, 2018.

Austin, Rachel, 'Self-Service Photography in Our Reading Rooms', *Living Knowledge Blog*, 19 December 2014, https://blogs.bl.uk/living-knowledge/ 2014/12/self-service-photography-in-our-reading-rooms.html.

Autin, Louis, 'The Nameless Crowds: Using Quantitative Data and Digital Tools to Study the Ancient Vocabulary of the Crowd in Tacitus', *Journal of Digital History*, 1, no. 1 (2021).

Baker, Nicholson, *Double Fold: Libraries and the Assault on Paper*. New York: Knopf Doubleday, 2001.

Barnet, Belinda, *Memory Machines: The Evolution of Hypertext*. London: Anthem, 2014.

Bennett, Sue, Karl Maton, and Lisa Kervin, 'The "Digital Natives" Debate: A Critical Review of the Evidence', *British Journal of Education Technology*, 39, no. 5 (August 2008), 775–86.

Binkley, Robert C., *Manual on Methods of Reproducing Research Materials*. Ann Arbor: Edwards Brothers, 1936.

Blevins, Cameron, 'Digital History's Perpetual Future Tense', in Matthew K. Gold and Lauren F. Klein (eds.), *Debates in the Digital Humanities 2016*. Minneapolis: University of Minnesota Press, 2016.

Blevins, Cameron, *Paper Trails: The US Post and the Making of the American West*. New York: Oxford University Press, 2021.

Blevins, Cameron and Richard W. Helbock, 'US Post Offices', 2021, https://cblevins.github.io/us-post-offices/.

Blevins, Cameron, Yan Wu, and Steven Braun, 'Gossamer Network', 2021, https://gossamernetwork.com.

Blouin Jr., Francis X. and William G. Rosenberg, *Processing the Past: Contesting Authority in History and the Archives*. Oxford: Oxford University Press, 2011.

Boutin, Paul, 'The Archivist', *Slate*, 7 April 2005, https://slate.com/technology/2005/04/the-internet-archive-wants-your-files.html.

Brennan, Sheila, 'My Digital Publishing Update: Nothing', *Lot49*, 4 June 2017, https://www.lotfortynine.org/2017/06/my-digital-publishing-update-nothing/.

Brennan, Sheila A., 'Public, First', in Matthew K. Gold and Lauren F. Klein (eds.), *Debates in the Digital Humanities 2016*. Minneapolis: University of Minnesota Press, 2016.

Brown, Laura, 'University Presses in the Age of COVID-19', *Ithaka S+R*, 24 June 2020, https://sr.ithaka.org/blog/university-presses-in-the-age-of-covid-19/.

Burgess, Anna, 'This Year, a Single Digitization Focus at Houghton', *Harvard Gazette*, 30 July 2020, https://news.harvard.edu/gazette/story/2020/07/houghtons-2020-21-digitization-focus-black-american-history/.

Bush, Vannevar, 'As We May Think', *The Atlantic*, July 1945, www.theatlantic.com/magazine/archive/1945/07/as-we-may-think/303881.

Callaci, Emily, 'On Acknowledgements', *American Historical Review*, 125, no. 1 (February 2020), 126–31.

'CHA Annual Meeting – Presentation', *ActiveHistory.ca*, 4 June 2009, http://activehistory.ca/2009/06/cha-annual-meeting-presentation/.

Chapman, Stephen, Paul Conway, and Anne R. Kenney, *Digital Imaging and Preservation Microfilm: The Future of the Hybrid Approach for the Preservation of Brittle Books*. Washington, DC: Council on Library and Information Resources, 1999.

Christen, Kimberly, 'Opening Archives: Respectful Repatriation', *American Archivist*, 74, no. 1 (Spring/Summer 2011), 185–210.

Clements, Jeff C., 'Open Access Articles Receive More Citations in Hybrid Marine Ecology Journals', *FACETS*, 2 (2017), 1–14.

Cohen, Daniel J. and Roy Rosenzweig, *Digital History: A Guide to Gathering, Preserving, and Presenting the Past on the Web*. Philadelphia: University of Pennsylvania Press, 2006.

Colutto, Sebastian, Philip Kahle, Hackl Guenter, and Guenter Muehlberger, 'Transkribus: A Platform for Automated Text Recognition and Searching of Historical Documents', in *2019 15th International Conference on eScience (eScience)*, 24–27 September 2019, 463–6.

Cook, Terry, 'The Archive(s) Is a Foreign Country: Historians, Archivists, and the Changing Archival Landscape', *Canadian Historical Review*, 90, no. 3 (September 2009), 497–534.

Corrado, Edward M. and Heather Lea Moulaison, *Digital Preservation for Libraries, Archives, and Museums*. Lanham: Rowman & Littlefield, 2014.

Crymble, Adam, *Technology and the Historian: Transformations in the Digital Age*. Urbana: University of Illinois Press, 2021.

'DigiLab: Putting Canada's History in Your Hands', *Library and Archives Canada*, 8 June 2016, https://www.bac-lac.gc.ca/eng/services-public/Pages/digilab.aspx.

Digital History Working Group, 'Guidelines for the Professional Evaluation of Digital Scholarship by Historians', *American Historical Association*, June 2015, www.historians.org/teaching-and-learning/digital-history-resources/ evaluation-of-digital-scholarship-in-history/guidelines-for-the-professional- evaluation-of-digital-scholarship-by-historians.

Eisenstein, Elizabeth, *The Printing Press as an Agent of Change*. Cambridge: Cambridge University Press, 1979.

'Emergency Temporary Access Service', *HathiTrust*, www.hathitrust.org/ ETAS-Description.

Eynon, Rebecca, 'The Myth of the Digital Native: Why it Persists and the Harm it Inflicts', in Tracey Burns and Francesca Gottschalk (eds.), *Education in the Digital Age: Healthy and Happy Children*. Paris: OECD, 2020, 131–43.

'FDR's Historic Campus Visit', *Queen's Alumni Review*, 13 August 2013, https:// www.queensu.ca/alumnireview/sites/alumnireview/files/2022-01/2013-3-QAR .pdf.

Fishbein, Meyer H., 'Introduction', in Meyer H. Fishbein (ed.), *The National Archives and Statistical Research*. Athens: Ohio University Press, 1973, xiii–xiv.

Fleckner, John, 'F. Gerald Ham: Jeremiah to the Profession', *American Archivist*, 77, no. 2 (October 2014), 377–93.

Fogel, Robert W. and Stanley L. Engerman, *Time on the Cross: The Economics of American Negro Slavery*. Boston: Little, Brown, 1974.

Frangou, Christina, 'The Growing Problem of Online Harassment in Academe', *University Affairs*, 23 October 2019, https://www.universityaffairs.ca/features/ feature-article/the-growing-problem-of-online-harassment-in-academe/.

Funk, Kellen and Lincoln A. Mullen, 'The Spine of American Law: Digital Text Analysis and U.S. Legal Practice', *American Historical Review*, 123, no. 1 (February 2018), 132–64. Dataset available on the Oxford University Press website for this article.

Fyfe, Paul, 'An Archeology of Victorian Newspapers', *Victorian Periodicals Review*, 49, no. 4 (Winter 2016), 546–77.

Gaule, Patrick and Nicholas Maystre, '*Getting Cited: Does Open Access Help?*', *Research Policy*, 40, no. 10 (2011), 1332–8.

Gavin, Michael, 'How to Think about EEBO', *Textual Cultures*, 11, no. 1–2 (2017), 70–105.

Geary, Patrick J., *Phantoms of Remembrance: Memory and Oblivion at the End of the First Millennium*. Princeton: Princeton University Press, 1994.

Germano, William, *Getting It Published: A Guide for Scholars and Anyone Else Serious about Serious Books*. Chicago: University of Chicago Press, 2016.

Gertz, Janet E., 'Microfilming for Archives and Manuscripts', *American Archivist*, 53, no. 2 (Spring 1990), 224–34.

Gibson, Abe, 'Keeping it Real: Historians in the Deepfake Era', *Perspectives on History*, 17 May 2021, https://www.historians.org/publications-and-directories/perspectives-on-history/may-2021/keeping-it-real-historians-in-the-deepfake-era.

Gitelman, Lisa, *Always Already New: Media, History, and the Data of Culture*. Cambridge, MA: MIT Press, 2008.

Gitelman, Lisa, *Paper Knowledge: Toward a Media History of Documents*. Durham: Duke University Press, 2014.

Gleick, James, *The Information: A History, a Theory, a Flood*. New York: Pantheon, 2011.

Graham, Shawn, Ian Milligan, and Scott Weingart, *Exploring Big Historical Data: The Historian's Macroscope*. London: Imperial College Press, 2016.

Graham, Shawn, Ian Milligan, and Scott Weingart, 'Writing the Historian's Macroscope in Public', *Perspectives on History*, 1 October 2014, https://www.historians.org/publications-and-directories/perspectives-on-history/october-2014/writing-the-historians-macroscope-in-public.

Gregg, Stephen H., *Old Books and Digital Publishing: Eighteenth-Century Collections Online*. Cambridge: Cambridge University Press, 2020.

Grove, Jack, 'Naomi Wolf's Dissertation – Public at Last', *Inside Higher Ed*, 29 April 2021, https://www.insidehighered.com/news/2021/04/29/naomi-wolf-dissertation-prompts-criticism-oxford#.YIrOwGgLUt0.twitter.

'Guidelines for Effective Knowledge Mobilization', *SSHRC*, 17 June 2019, https://www.sshrc-crsh.gc.ca/funding-financement/policies-politiques/knowledge_mobilisation-mobilisation_des_connaissances-eng.aspx.

Guldi, Jo, 'Critical Search: A Procedure for Guided Reading in Large-Scale Textual Corpora', *Journal of Cultural Analytics*, 3, no. 1 (2018).

Guldi, Jo and David Armitage, *The History Manifesto*. Cambridge: Cambridge University Press, 2014.

Hafner, Katie, 'In Challenge to Google, Yahoo Will Scan Books', *New York Times*, 3 October 2005, C1, https://www.nytimes.com/2005/10/03/business/in-challenge-to-google-yahoo-will-scan-books.html.

Hattem, Michael D., 'Debating the History Dissertation Embargo Policy at the Annual Meeting', *Perspectives on History*, 5 February 2015, https://www.historians.org/publications-and-directories/perspectives-on-history/february-2015/debating-the-history-dissertation-embargo-policy-at-the-annual-meeting.

Hitchcock, Tim, 'Confronting the Digital: Or How Academic History Writing Lost the Plot', *Cultural and Social History*, 10, no. 1 (2013), 9–23.

Hitchcock, Tim and William J. Turkel, 'The Old Bailey Proceedings, 1674–1913: Text Mining for Evidence of Court Behavior', *Law and History Review*, 34, no. 4 (2016), 929–55.

Hogge, Becky, 'Becky Hogge on the Egghead Who Hopes to Create a Permanent Record of All Human Knowledge', *New Statesman*, 17 October 2005, https://www.newstatesman.com/long-reads/2005/10/brewster-kahle.

Jenkins, Keith, *Rethinking History*. London: Routledge, 1991.

Johns, Adrian, *Piracy: The Intellectual Property Wars from Gutenberg to Gates*. Chicago: University of Chicago Press, 2009.

Jones, Esyllt W., Shelley Sweeney, Ian Milligan, Greg Bak, and Jo-Anne McCutcheon, 'Remembering is a Form of Honouring: Preserving the COVID-19 Archival Record', *FACETS*, 6, no. 1 (April 2021), 545–68.

Jordanova, Ludmilla, *History in Practice*, 3rd ed. London: Bloomsbury, 2019.

Joyce, Patrick, *Visions of the People: Industrial England and the Question of Class, c.1848–1914*. Cambridge: Cambridge University Press, 1991.

Kahle, Brewster, 'All Icelandic Literature to Go Online?', *Internet Archive Blog*, 29 January 2011, http://blog.archive.org/2011/01/29/all-icelandic-literature-to-go-online/.

Kahle, Brewster, 'Digitizing All Balinese Literature', *Internet Archive Blog*, 30 January 2011, http://blog.archive.org/2011/01/30/digitizing-all-balinese-literature/.

Kahle, Brewster, 'Microfilm: The Rise, Fall, and New Life of Microfilm Collections', 14 December 2020, https://archive.org/details/reading-of-microfilm-the-rise-fall-and-new-life-of-microfilm-collections.

Katz, Michael, *The People of Hamilton, Canada West: Family and Class in a Mid-Nineteenth-Century City*. Cambridge, MA: Harvard University Press, 1975.

Katz, Stan, 'Publishing History Digitally', *Chronicle of Higher Education Blogs*, 11 May 2010, https://web.archive.org/web/20170824153530/https:/chronicle.com/blogs/brainstorm/publishing-history-digitally/23894.

Kelly, Kevin, 'Scan This Book!', *New York Times*, 14 May 2006, https://www.nytimes.com/2006/05/14/magazine/14publishing.html.

'Kevin Kruse's Twitter Profile', *Twitter.com*, https://twitter.com/KevinMKruse.

Kirschenbaum, Matthew and Sarah Werner, 'Digital Scholarship and Digital Studies: The State of the Discipline', *Book History*, 17 (2014), 406–58.

Kuhn, Virginia and Anke Finger (eds.), *Shaping the Digital Dissertation*. Cambridge: Open Book, 2021.

Lebert, Marie, *Project Gutenberg (1971–2008)*. Project Gutenberg eBook, 2008, www.gutenberg.org/ebooks/27045.

Lemercier, Claire and Claire Zalc, *Quantitative Methods in the Humanities: An Introduction*, trans. Arthur Goldhammer. Charlottesville: University of Virginia Press, 2019.

Leon, Sharon, 'Complicating a "Great Man" Narrative of Digital History in the United States', in Elizabeth Losh and Jacqueline Wernimont (eds.), *Bodies of Information: Intersectional Feminism and Digital Humanities*. Minneapolis: University of Minnesota Press, 2018.

Library and Archives Canada, 'Self-Serve Digital Copying Pilot Project', *Internet Archive Wayback Machine*, 1 November 2005, https://web.archive.org/web/20060211042512/http://www.collectionscanada.ca/services/005-211-e.html.

'List of Fonds and Collections', *Library and Archives Canada*, www.bac-lac.gc.ca/eng/discover/archives-literary/Pages/list-fonds-collections.aspx.

Locke, Joseph L. and Ben Wright, 'History Can Be Open Source: Democratic Dreams and the Rise of Digital History', *American Historical Review*, 126, no. 4 (December 2021), 1485–511.

Luther, Frederic, *Microfilm: A History, 1839–1900*. Annapolis: National Microfilm Association, 1959.

Madrigal, Alexis C., 'The Way We Write History Has Changed', *The Atlantic*, 21 January 2020, https://www.theatlantic.com/technology/archive/2020/01/smartphone-archives-history-photography/605284/.

Maemura, Emily, Nicholas Worby, Ian Milligan, and Christoph Becker, 'If These Crawls Could Talk: Studying and Documenting Web Archives Provenance', *Journal of the Association for Information Science and Technology*, 69, no. 10 (October 2018), 1223–33.

Marcum, Deanna and Roger C. Schonfeld, *Along Came Google: A History of Library Digitization*. Princeton: Princeton University Press, 2021.

Marius, Richard and Melvin Page, *A Short Guide to Writing about History*, 9th ed. New York: Pearson, 2014.

Massot, Marie-Laure, Arianna Sforzini, and Vincent Ventresque, 'Transcribing Foucault's Handwriting with Transkribus', *Journal of Data Mining and Digital Humanities* (2019), https://jdmdh.episciences.org/5218/pdf.

McCall, Jenny and Amy Bourke-Waite, 'The Academic Book of the Future and the Need to Break Boundaries', in Rebecca E. Lyons and Samantha J. Rayner (eds.), *The Academic Book of the Future*. Basingstoke: Palgrave Macmillan, 2016, 32–8.

McDaniel, W. Caleb, 'Open Notebook History', 22 May 2013, http://wcaleb .org/blog/open-notebook-history.

Michel, Jean-Baptiste, Yuan Kui Shen, Aviva Presser Aiden et al., 'Quantitative Analysis of Culture Using Millions of Digitized Books', *Science*, 331, no. 6014 (January 2011), 176–82.

Millar, Laura A., *A Matter of Facts: The Value of Evidence in an Information Age*. Chicago: ALA Neal-Schuman, 2019.

Milligan, Ian, *History in the Age of Abundance? How the Web is Transforming Historical Research*. Montreal: McGill-Queen's University Press, 2019.

Milligan, Ian, 'Illusionary Order: Online Databases and the Changing Foundation of Canadian Historiography, 1997–2010', *Canadian Historical Review*, 94, no. 4 (December 2013), 540–69.

Milligan, Ian, 'Mining the "Internet Graveyard": Rethinking the Historians' Toolkit', *Journal of the Canadian Historical Association*, 23, no. 2 (2012), 21–64.

Milligan, Ian, 'We Are All Digital Now: Digital Photography and the Reshaping of Historical Practice', *Canadian Historical Review*, 101, no. 4 (December 2020), 602–21.

Mills, Alexandra, 'User Impact on Selection, Digitization, and the Development of Digital Special Collections', *New Review of Academic Librarianship*, 21, no. 2 (2015), 160–9.

Munslow, Alun, *The New History*. Harlow: Longman, 2003.

'The National Archives: A Pioneer in Microfilm', *Google Arts & Culture*, https://artsandculture.google.com/exhibit/the-national-archives-a-pioneer-in-microfilm-u-s-national-archives/QQXzWF8K?hl=en.

National Archives of Ireland, 'Using the Reading Room', 2021, https://www .nationalarchives.ie/visit-us/using-the-reading-room/.

Noble, Safiya, *Algorithms of Oppression: How Search Engines Reinforce Racism*. New York: New York University Press, 2018.

Novick, Peter, *That Noble Dream: The 'Objectivity Question' and the American Historical Profession*. Cambridge: Cambridge University Press, 1988.

O'Neill, Cathy, *Weapons of Math Destruction: How Big Data Increases Inequality and Threatens Democracy*. New York: Penguin Random House, 2016.

O'Shea, Lizzie, *Future Histories: What Ada Lovelace, Tom Paine, and the Paris Commune Can Teach Us about Digital Technology*. London: Verso, 2019.

Oberbichler, Sarah and Eva Pfanzelter, 'Topic-Specific Corpus Building: A Step Towards a Representative Newspaper Corpus on the Topic of Return Migration Using Text Mining Methods', *Journal of Digital History*, 1, no. 1 (2021).

Palmer, Bryan D., *Descent Into Discourse: The Reification of Language and the Writing of Social History*. Philadelphia: Temple University Press, 1990.

Parker, Geoffrey, 'Braudel's "Mediterranean": The Making and Marketing of a Masterpiece', *History*, 59, no. 196 (1974), 238–43.

Peace, Thomas, 'New Methods, New Schools, New Stories: Digital Archives and Dartmouth's Institutional Legacy', in Ivy Schweitzer and Gordon Henry (eds.), *Afterlives of Indigenous Archives*. Hanover: Dartmouth College Press, 2019, 95–119.

Peace, Thomas, 'Rethinking Access to the Past: History and Archives in the Digital Age', *Acadiensis*, 48, no. 2 (Autumn 2019), 217–29.

Power, Eugene B. with Robert Anderson, *Edition of One: The Autobiography of Eugene B. Power, Founder of University Microfilms*. Ann Arbor: University Microfilm International, 1990.

Putnam, Lara, 'The Transnational and the Text-Searchable: Digitized Sources and the Shadows They Cast', *American Historical Review*, 121, no. 2 (April 2016), 377–402.

Rabb, Theodore K., 'The Development of Quantification in Historical Research', *Journal of Interdisciplinary History*, 13, no. 4 (1983), 591–601.

'Research Data Archiving Policy', *SSHRC*, 9 December 2016, https://www.sshrc-crsh.gc.ca/about-au_sujet/policies-politiques/statements-enonces/edata-donnees_electroniques-eng.aspx.

Research Excellence Framework 2021, 'Guidance on Submissions', January 2019, https://www.ref.ac.uk/publications/guidance-on-submissions-201901/.

Richardson, Heather Cox, 'Letters from an American', *SubStack*, https://heathercoxrichardson.substack.com.

Robertson, Stephen, 'The Differences between Digital Humanities and Digital History', in Matthew K. Gold and Lauren F. Klein (eds.), *Debates in the Digital Humanities 2016*. Minneapolis: University of Minnesota Press, 2016.

Robertson, Stephen and Lincoln Mullen, 'Arguing with Digital History: Patterns of Historical Interpretation', *Journal of Social History*, 54, no. 4 (2021), 1005–22.

Robertson, Tara, 'digitization: just because you can, doesn't mean you should', *Tara Robertson Consulting*, 20 March 2016, https://tararobertson.ca/2016/oob/.

Romein, C. Annemieke, Max Kemman, Julie M. Birkholz et al., 'State of the Field: Digital History', *History: The Journal of the Historical Association*, 105, no. 365 (2020), 291–312.

Rosenzweig, Roy, 'Scarcity or Abundance? Preserving the Past in a Digital Era', *American Historical Review*, 108, no. 3 (June 2003), 735–62.

Rutner, Jennifer and Roger C. Schonfeld, 'Supporting the Changing Research Practices of Historians', *Ithaka S + R*, 10 December 2012, https://www.sr .ithaka.org/sites/all/modules/contrib/pubdlcnt/pubdlcnt.php?file=http://www .sr.ithaka.org/sites/default/files/reports/supporting-the-changing-research-prac tices-of-historians.pdf&nid=532.

Schlottmann, Kevin, 'Updating Finding Aids during the 2020 COVID Shutdown', *Columbia's Rare Book & Manuscript Library*, 13 January 2021, https://blogs.cul.columbia.edu/rbml/2021/01/13/updating-finding-aids-during-the-2020-covid-shutdown/.

Selwyn, Neil, 'The Digital Native – Myth and Reality', *Aslib Proceedings*, 61, no. 4 (July 2009), 364–79.

Shirky, Clay, *Cognitive Surplus: Creativity and Generosity in a Connected Age*. Google eBook. New York: Penguin, 2010.

Smyth, Hannah and Diego Ramirez Echavarria, 'Twitter and Feminist Commemoration of the 1916 Easter Rising', *Journal of Digital History*, 1, no. 1 (2021).

Somin, Ilya, 'University Presses Shouldn't Have to Make a Profit', *The Atlantic*, 11 May 2019, https://www.theatlantic.com/ideas/archive/2019/05/why-cuts-stanford-university-press-are-wrong/589219/.

St. Onge, Anna, 'Collaboration between Archivists and Historians: Finding a Middle Ground', *ActiveHistory.ca*, 29 June 2017, https://activehistory.ca/ 2017/06/collaboration-between-archivists-and-historians-finding-a-middle-ground/.

Steig, Margaret F., 'The Information Needs of Historians', *College and Research Libraries*, 42, no. 6 (1981), 549–60.

Storey, William Kelleher and Towser Jones, *Writing History: A Guide for Canadian Students*. Toronto: Oxford University Press, 2007.

Sullivan, Elaine A., *Constructing the Sacred: Visibility and Ritual Landscape at the Egyptian Necropolis of Saqqara*. Palo Alto: Stanford University Press, 2020, https://constructingthesacred.org.

Swierenga, Robert P., 'Clio and Computers: A Survey of Computerized Research in History', *Computers and the Humanities*, 5, no. 1 (September 1970), 1–21.

Tanner, Simon, 'Deciding Whether Optical Character Recognition Is Feasible', *King's Digital Consultancy Services*, December 2004, https://www.kb.nl/sites/default/files/docs/OCRFeasibility_final.pdf.

Terras, Melissa, 'Crowdsourcing in the Digital Humanities', in Susan Schreibman, Ray Siemens, and John Unsworth (eds.), *A New Companion to Digital Humanities*. Hoboken: Wiley-Blackwell, 2016, 420–39.

Terras, Melissa, Julianne Nyhan, and Edward Vanhoutte (eds.), *Defining Digital Humanities: A Reader*. London: Routledge, 2013.

Theimer, Kate, 'Archives in Context and as Context', *Journal of Digital Humanities*, 1, no. 2 (Spring 2012), http://journalofdigitalhumanities.org/1-2/archives-in-context-and-as-context-by-kate-theimer/.

Thompson, Samantha, 'Why Don't Archivists Digitize Everything?', *ARCHIVES @ PAMA Blog*, 31 May 2017, https://peelarchivesblog.com/2017/05/31/why-dont-archivists-digitize-everything/.

Tilton, Lauren, 'On Tenure in Digital History', *Perspectives on History*, 20 May 2019, https://www.historians.org/publications-and-directories/perspectives-on-history/may-2019/on-tenure-in-digital-history.

Tosh, John, *The Pursuit of History: Aims, Methods and New Directions in the Study of History*, 6th ed. London: Routledge, 2015.

Turchin, Peter, 'Arise "cliodynamics"', *Nature*, 454 (2008), 34–5.

Underwood, Ted, 'Theorizing Research Practices We Forgot to Theorize Twenty Years Ago', *Representations*, 127, no. 1 (Summer 2014), 64–72.

Varin, Vanessa, 'The Dos and Don'ts of Live-Tweeting at an Academic Conference: A Working Draft', *Perspectives on History*, 12 February 2013, https://www.historians.org/publications-and-directories/perspectives-on-history/february-2013/the-dos-and-donts-of-live-tweeting-at-an-academic-conference-a-working-draft.

Vreede, Triparna de, Cuong Nguyen, Gert-Jan de Vreede et al., 'A Theoretical Model of User Engagement in Crowdsourcing', in Pedro Antunes, Marco Aurélio Gerosa, Allan Sylvester, Julita Vassileva, and Gert-Jan Vreede (eds.), *Collaboration and Technology, CRIWG 2013*. Lecture Notes in Computer Science, 8224, 30 October–1 November 2013, 94–109.

Walsham, Alexandra, 'The Social History of the Archive: Record-Keeping in Early Modern Europe', *Past and Present*, 230, no. supplement 11 (November 2016), 9–48.

Weller, Toni (ed.), *History in the Digital Age*. New York: Routledge, 2013.

'What is Minimal Computing?', 2014, https://go-dh.github.io/mincomp/about/.

Whitehouse, Harvey, Pieter François, Patrick E. Savage et al., 'Complex Societies Precede Moralizing Gods Throughout World History', *Nature*, 568 (2019), 226–9.

'Who We Are', *The Conversation Canada*, https://theconversation.com/ca/who-we-are.

Widiadana, Rita A. and Ni Komang Erviani, 'Ancient "Lontar" Manuscripts Go Digital', *Jakarta Post*, 29 January 2011, https://web.archive.org/web/20110129195542/http://www.thejakartapost.com/news/2011/01/29/ancient-'lontar'-manuscripts-go-digital.html.

Wieringa, Jeri E., 'Modeling the Religious Culture of Seventh-Day Adventism, 1843–1920', Unpublished Doctoral Dissertation, George Mason University, Summer 2019, http://dissertation.jeriwieringa.com.

Winling, LaDale, 'Getting Tenure with Digital History', *Perspectives on History*, 8 April 2019, https://www.historians.org/publications-and-directories/perspectives-on-history/april-2019/getting-tenure-with-digital-history-how-one-scholar-made-his-case.

Wrigley, Edward Anthony, *Population and History*. London: Weidenfeld & Nicolson, 1969.

Acknowledgements

My sincerest thanks to those who made this Element possible. Special thanks to Professor Daniel Woolf, who first approached me with the idea of writing for this series and then provided indispensable feedback as the project developed. The two anonymous readers did a fabulous job of providing encouraging yet critical feedback. I would also like to thank my friend and colleague Thomas Peace for taking the time to read and comment on this manuscript. Audiences at Queen's University, the Université de Moncton, and the Oxford Internet Institute heard portions of this manuscript. Their questions and comments helped to strengthen it. Finally, I would like to thank my family: Jenn, Auden, and Isla. Thanks to the power of digital archives, I don't need to be in far-flung reading rooms, and I can spend less time on the road and more time at home. At the end of the day, that's a win!

Cambridge Elements ≡

Historical Theory and Practice

Daniel Woolf
Queen's University, Ontario

Daniel Woolf is Professor of History at Queen's University, where he served for ten years as Principal and Vice-Chancellor, and has held academic appointments at a number of Canadian universities. He is the author or editor of several books and articles on the history of historical thought and writing, and on early modern British intellectual history, including most recently *A Concise History of History* (CUP 2019). He is a Fellow of the Royal Historical Society, the Royal Society of Canada, and the Society of Antiquaries of London. He is married with 3 adult children.

About the Series
Cambridge Elements in Historical Theory and Practice is a series intended for a wide range of students, scholars, and others whose interests involve engagement with the past. Topics include the theoretical, ethical, and philosophical issues involved in doing history, the interconnections between history and other disciplines and questions of method, and the application of historical knowledge to contemporary global and social issues such as climate change, reconciliation and justice, heritage, and identity politics.

Cambridge Elements ≡

Historical Theory and Practice

Printed in the United States
by Baker & Taylor Publisher Services